Praise for Cy Charney and
The Salesperson's Handbook

"Charney has a knack for writing that makes his books easy to read and practical. The checklist format is wonderful — it takes less than 60 seconds to get the information you need. This is a must-have for all people in sales."

— PETER URS BENDER, bestselling author of
Leadership from Within, *Secrets of Power Presentations*,
Secrets of Power Marketing, and
Secrets of Face-to-Face Communication.

"A thorough 'basics' book for anyone in sales — and who isn't?"

— ALAN C. MIDDLETON, PH.D., executive director,
Division of Executive Development,
Schulich School of Business, York University

"A very strong foundation for sales professionals who are serious about their careers."

— IAN SELBIE, President,
PowerMarketing, Vancouver

"Charney has created the consummate handbook for today's sales professional. *The Salesperson's Handbook* is a practical resource that will help build and maintain profitable customer relationships."

— RHONDA L. ELTON, Vice President and General Manager,
Mobile Power, Xantrex Technology

The Salesperson's Handbook

The Salesperson's Handbook

Cy Charney

Published in Canada in 2002 by
Stoddart Publishing Co. Limited
895 Don Mills Road, 400-2 Park Centre, Toronto, Canada M3C 1W3

Published in the United States in 2003 by
Stoddart Publishing Co. Limited
PMB 128, 4500 Witmer Estates, Niagara Falls, New York 14305-1386

To order Stoddart books please contact General Distribution Services
In Canada Tel. (416) 213-1919   Fax (416) 213-1917
Email cservice@genpub.com
In the United States Toll-free tel. 1-800-805-1083 Toll-free fax 1-800-481-6207
Email gdsinc@genpub.com

www.stoddartpub.com

10   9   8   7   6   5   4   3   2   1

National Library of Canada Cataloguing in Publication Data

Charney, Cyril
The salesperson's handbook
Includes index.

0-7737-6280-9
1. Selling.   I. Title.

HF5438.25.C555   2002   658.85   C2002-900588-4

U.S. Cataloging-in-Publication Data Available from the Publisher

Cover design: Bill Douglas at The Bang
Text design: Tannice Goddard
Typesetting: Kinetics Design & Illustration

THE CANADA COUNCIL | LE CONSEIL DES ARTS
FOR THE ARTS | DU CANADA
SINCE 1957 | DEPUIS 1957

*We acknowledge for their financial support of our publishing program the Canada Council,
the Ontario Arts Council, and the Government of Canada through the
Book Publishing Industry Development Program (BPIDP).*

Printed and bound in Canada

Sometimes I'm stubborn.
I usually hog the remote control.
I can't spell to save my life.
I don't always call when I should.
I often neglect those I should spend more time with.
My listening skills don't even measure on any scale of acceptability.

So, I dedicate this book to all those who accept me as I am,
And more so to those who love me.

Contents

Preface

$\mathcal{T}$his book is for all salespeople. It makes no assumptions about you, your background, or your industry. It does presume that you want to be more successful. And it provides you with a quick resource guide to help you get to the next level.

Since salespeople come from a variety of industries, all of which operate differently, this book offers help to those who are

- single-cycle selling
- focusing on meeting customer needs
- developing long-term strategic relationships

By organizing principles into short chapters and categories, the reader/learner will be able to access information quickly, putting them into practice and achieving results.

Acknowledgements

$\mathcal{T}$o ensure that *The Salesperson's Handbook* is relevant to the needs of salespeople today, I sought the advice of a variety of people in the field. These mentors have made an invaluable contribution to the book through their valuable suggestions:

Marc Charlebois, general sales manager of Team 1050 CHUM and 104.5 CHUM FM, Toronto

Elise Jankelow, director of sales, Compugen Inc., Markham

Nahla Hanna, vice-president, sales, AON Reed Stenhouse Inc., Toronto

Max Lissoos, vice-president, sales, Global Materials Technologies Inc., Chicago

Ken Imrie, national sales coach, IBM, Canada

Jack Kahan, retired district manager, QSP Inc. (Subsidiary of Reader's Digest), Toronto

Irwin Katz, sales and marketing consultant

Michelle Hiltz, sales representative

Nick Garrison, freelance editor

Sue Sumeraj, editor

Introduction

Meeting Customers' Needs

*There is only one boss: the customer.
And he can fire everybody in the company, from
the chairman on down, simply by
spending his money somewhere else.*

SAM WALTON, FOUNDER OF WAL-MART

Customers are our reason for being. They pay our bills and salaries, and allow us to stay in business. It is imperative, therefore, that we understand what customers need so that we can meet those needs.

These are most important needs that customers have:

1. **Reliability.** Customers want you to meet your obligations. They want what was promised, when it was promised. Maybe more, but not less!

2. **Speed.** It's not a question of months. It's not an issue of weeks, or even days. Things need to be done right away. Yesterday would be even better. Speed is a major competitive advantage.

Salespeople can demonstrate that they understand the customer's sense of urgency by

- returning phone calls within the hour
- responding to e-mails at least twice daily
- submitting their order, on-line, immediately
- maintaining paperwork

Electronic, wireless communication tools can enable you to respond quickly and accurately.

3. **Empathy.** You cannot satisfy everyone all of the time. But, you can put yourself in their shoes and understand their frustration or disappointment or anger. Let them know you understand. Then tell them what you will do to reduce their level of frustration.

4. **Knowledge.** Knowledge brings respect. It enables you to provide answers and solve problems quickly. It also enhances your ability to sway customers by increasing your influence.

5. **Tangibility.** The physical appearance of everything associated with you and your organization sends messages related to attractiveness, neatness, and worth. This applies to your product, premises, dress and everything else that the customer can see and feel.

6. **Value.** People don't mind paying more if they feel they are getting more. The more reliable, quick, and courteous you are, relative to your competitors, the more you can charge.

Remind yourself daily of your customers' needs. Whenever you have an unsuccessful meeting, determine which of your customer's needs you neglected the most. Learn from the experience and do better on your next call.

A formula for failure is simple: anticipate what your prospect wants *before* you have found out. Never give prospects any information *before* you have established their needs.

Each customer will have a different priority of needs. For some, it will be value. For others, it will be speed. Although all are important, your probing will establish the current hot button and enable you to customize your approach each time, thereby increasing your ability to be successful.

Each customer has these basic human needs:
- the need to feel safe (psychologically, socially and physically)
- the need to be treated as special
- the need to feel successful
- the need to have things done right the first time
- the need to get things done efficiently

Offering to meet these needs will increase your sales.

THE CUSTOMERS' BILL OF RIGHTS

1. Customer are stakeholders in our organization. They are the most important of the three (the other two being the shareholders and the staff).

2. Customers are different and unique. Each needs to be treated individually.

3. Customers are not dependent on us. We are dependent on them.

4. Customers deserve value. Every process in our organization must have a direct or indirect value to our customers, be they internal or external. Processes that don't add value should be eliminated or reduced.

5. Customers have needs and wants. Our job is to find out what they are and fulfill them.

6. Customers should expect to get our individual attention.

7. Customers are not an interruption to our work, but the reason for our work.

8. Customers pay our bills.

9. Customers want someone to be loyal to — a trusted and respected partner.

10. Customers reign supreme.

KEY POINT:

The cost of acquiring a new customer is five times more than the cost of serving your existing customers.

Planning and Managing Your Territory

Plans are nothing; planning is everything

Dwight D. Eisenhower (1890–1969), 34th President of the United States

Assuming that you have taken over a new territory, here are strategies you can use to manage the new area and its customers effectively:

1. Analyze the existing situation. Interview people who have managed the territory before to gain their assessment. Find out what has been effective in the past in terms of money, people, and time, and the benefits derived as a consequence. Look for change in terms of
   - overall sales
   - gross margins
   - market share
   - trends

2. Find out how performance was influenced by
   - segmentation of the territory
   - your organization's strengths and weaknesses
   - any external factors

3. Look to the future. Forecast the performance you expect. You can do this by

- extrapolating past performance into the future
- looking at new economic data that might cause a change in the ongoing performance

4. Set goals. Ensure that your goals are SMART, that is,

- **S** pecific
- **M** easurable
- **A** greed upon by all stakeholders
- **R** ealistic
- **T** ime-based

and challenging, too.

5. The goals can cover many aspects of your territory. They can, for example, include

- sales, such as
  - increased sales to existing customers
  - sales to new customers
  - increased margins
  - cost changes
  - product mix changes
- product development, such as
  - the number of new products/services introduced
  - the penetration of the total mix that the new items constitute
- customer development, such as
  - the number of new accounts opened
  - the penetration of the total accounts that the new accounts constitute

6. Plans are made to achieve the goals. They should state what actions are to be taken, when, by whom, and who needs to be informed/consulted on actions that are outside of the salesperson's jurisdiction.

7. Measure changes to ensure that benefits are being realized. To do so, identify the key indicators of performance. These could, for example, include
- sales indicators
  - dollar sales
  - unit sales
  - order to call ratio
  - market share
- promotions
  - number of new accounts
  - number of referrals
  - number of new accounts lured away from the competition
- effectiveness
  - percentage of time spent with clients
  - percentage of time spent on travel
  - change in expenses
  - timeliness of reports
  - accuracy of reports

People, Politics, and Organizations:

Who Has the Influence?

*If you're going to play the game properly,
you'd better know every rule.*

BARBARA JORDAN, AMERICAN LAWYER, POLITICIAN

Organizations are highly complex places. There are many people whose opinions and actions can affect your ability to be influential in their organization. In developing a strategy to be effective over the long term, it is important to know who they are and find a way of cultivating relationships with them. The more they value you, the less likely you will be "blocked" from ongoing and painless sales.

1. These are the key players to build relationships with:
- *The Buyer.* This is the person who signs the order.
- *Decision-makers.* These people have the power to OK or veto a sale. The buyer merely presents her recommendations to the decision-makers for approval.
- *Users.* These are the internal customers of the buyer and decision-makers. They are the end-users, including the engineers, programmers, line managers, and other front-line staff.

- *Gatekeepers.* These people work directly with the buyer in a support capacity. They include switchboard, secretarial, and administrative support staff. Calls are often routed to them before the buyer. As such, their attitudes can have a major impact on your ability to communicate directly with the buyer.
- *Influencers.* These people possess the technical knowledge to evaluate the effectiveness of your product or service.

2. Spend time developing an understanding of how decisions are made inside your major account organizations.

3. Rank the key people in order of importance (influence). Prioritize your time so that you spend 80 percent of it developing relationships with the few people who really matter to your business.

4. Try to learn more about key contacts, such as
- family details (including names)
- special interests
- hobbies
- birthdays
- years of service in the company
- career ambitions

5. Enter your data into your database system. Retrieve it as you prepare for each meeting (in person or by phone).

6. Make a point of using your information at all points of contact to demonstrate your interest.

7. Stay in touch with satisfied clients by

- sending them cards for special occasions such as birthdays or anniversaries of when they became your clients
- sending them articles that you believe would be of interest to them
- updating them on new uses for your products or services
- following up to ensure that the product/service is meeting their expectations
- informing them of new developments in the field
- sending a handwritten note after all significant sales

1

Prospecting

Prospecting Overview

*Sales are contingent upon the attitude of the salesman –
not the attitude of the prospect.*

W. CLEMENT STONE, AMERICAN BUSINESSMAN

*P*rospecting is the key to your success. Your success today is a result of the prospecting you did six months ago. Make sure that you prospect every day by making cold calls, advertising, following up on hot leads, networking, speaking or writing. Get out there and ensure your future by planting seeds daily.

1. There are two reasons to look for new prospects:
- to increase sales
- to replace customers who, for one reason or another, are lost over time

2. An ideal prospect is a person who has the authority, potential, and desire to buy your product or service.

3. Prospects for different industries and trades are to be found in different places. For example:
- real estate salespeople may find prospects in local hotels
- industrial products salespeople may look in industry directories or trade shows
- sellers of training might find prospects at training association meetings

4. The most common methods of prospecting are
- cold canvassing
- referrals
- public exhibitions
- strategic partners
- direct mail
- telephone and telemarketing
- observation
- networking

5. In order to prospect most effectively, you should
- not rely on any one method exclusively
- change your approach if your chosen method is not providing the results aimed for

6. Salespeople who are effective in prospecting always prioritize their opportunities, taking the most important prospects first, and follow up regularly until their timing coincides with the decision to commit.

Twelve Great Ideas
to Increase Sales

We are what we repeatedly do.
Excellence, then, is not an act but a habit.

ARISTOTLE (384–22 BC), GREEK PHILOSPHER

1. Adopt orphan accounts. Often, due to the natural turnover of
salespeople in an organization, you will find accounts falling
between the cracks and being under-serviced. Jump in quickly
to fill the gap and ensure continuity of service.

2. Constantly ask for feedback anytime you are not successful. Learn
from your mistakes and improve your techniques and strategies.

3. When you are successful, think about what you did right. Then
do whatever you can to repeat the good feelings, thoughts, and
techniques that you used.

4. Be persistent, but not annoying. Research shows that 70 percent
of sales are made after the fifth contact.

5. Be passionate about your product or service. After all, if you're not, why should anyone else be?

6. Never be afraid to ask for the order. The potential buyer knows you want the order, you know it, so when you get a buying signal, close the sale!

7. Always ensure that each sale will endear you to the buyer. At the end of each transaction, the buyer should feel happy to have dealt with you.

8. Confirm that the buyer has gotten the satisfaction she was looking for. Follow up to show your interest and if possible listen for clues that more orders are on the way.

9. Ask a satisfied buyer for names of other people who might derive the same benefits as she has.

10. Have multiple contacts at your key accounts to ensure continuity if someone leaves.

11. Be a resource to your contacts. Be helpful with advice that may not lead to sales immediately, but which will generate goodwill and appreciation.

12. Love what you do. When you stop loving your work, take a break or look for another way to make a living.

Sales Letters

The finest eloquence is that which gets things done.

DAVID LLOYD GEORGE (1863–1945),
PRIME MINISTER OF GREAT BRITAIN

People are inundated with junk mail and other irritating communications. Their attention span has become very short. Attracting potential buyers through letters and bulk e-mail is a real art. This chapter will provide clues on how to dramatically increase your chances of a response.

1. Target your mailing. Generalized mailings get few responses. Ensure that your message appeals to a narrow audience. If necessary, customize different mailings for subcategories of potential buyers/users.

2. Write your letter so that it appears to be customized for each person. If your letter is too general, it will have little appeal. Readers should feel that it was specifically written to them.

Example of a personal letter:

Dear _____ ,

*Thank you for your request for a price on our model.
I am delighted by your interest in this product — it shows
sound judgement! I am attaching your quotation and
have sent, under separate cover, a catalogue with
supporting information.*

*As you are a valued client, I want to assist you in any
way that I can. Please contact me at any time by phone,
fax, or e-mail so that I can give you the personal attention
you deserve.*

3. A good introduction is critical. Grab the reader's attention quickly.
You have seconds between the moment the reader opens the letter
and the moment when he decides what to do with it so ensure
that the first impression is powerful. Consider starting with
- a controversial heading
- a challenging question
- a controversial picture
- an appeal to a fundamental urge, such as fear, greed,
  quiet, a need for exclusivity, a desire for love or beauty

4. Cater to both "skimmers" and "readers." Highlight in bold or
colour to give skimmers the flavour of the message. But offer
sufficient depth of information for readers, who want details
before making a decision to go to the next step.

5. Keep the message short. People have limited attention spans, particularly if they have a pile of mail to read through. Eliminate any redundant information that fails to enhance the message.

6. Provide comprehensive information. This objective may conflict with your attempts to keep the message short. Aim for a balance. Remember that long messages are acceptable when they are useful and interesting.

7. Talk to your reader. Your reader should almost be able to imagine you sitting next to him and discussing the issues. To achive a conversational writing style, you may start some sentences with "and" or "but" and end the odd sentence with a preposition. You might even use a fragmented sentence to highlight or emphasize.

8. Provide proof that your product or service is as good as you say it is. Back up your self-praise with statistics and testimonials that deal with key issues of sceptics.

9. Give something free, for example
   - a sample
   - a money-back guarantee
   - a trial at a reduced cost
   - an information booklet
   - a trial offer
   - cost-saving for a certain period
   - an opportunity to be part of a contest or draw

But ensure that the offer does not cheapen the product or service. For example, ask for something in return such as using the client for future testimonials.

10. Develop rapport. Treat the reader as if you're on the same team.
- As much as possible, use "we" or "you" in place of "I."
  For example:
  "We both know that . . ."
- Pay compliments. For example:
  "People with your reputation . . . "

11. Use strong positive language. Use "will" rather than "could," "can," or "should."

12. Create motivation for the reader to act. Consider
- imposing a deadline:
  "This offer expires on . . ."
- offering limited quantities:
  "This offer is available for the first 10 callers . . ."

13. Make it easy for the reader to contact you. Provide
- a postpaid reply envelope
- a toll-free telephone number
- your e-mail address

14. Use a reference letter to add credibility to your message. The better known the organization and the higher the position of the author, the more effective it will be.

15. Increase the chances of your envelope being opened by using envelopes that are high quality, closed-faced, and size 10. Avoid the use of envelopes with labels, postage metering, illustrations, teaser copy, and corporate logos.

16. Use teaser copy on the envelope only if it directs the potential reader to a benefit. For example: "Page 2 will give you 3 free ways to cut taxes by a minimum of 10%!" Avoid teaser copy that gives away the whole story. For example: "Your accountant will wish he got this first!"

17. Keep it simple.
- Stay away from jargon, words with double meanings, or words that people seldom use.
- Of every 100 words, aim to have 70 or more of one or two syllables. If this is difficult, look for alternative words in a thesaurus.
- Keep paragraphs to six lines or fewer.
- Use short, snappy sentences of no more than 20 words.
- Keep your use of commas to a minimum.
- Don't use "and" where you could use a period instead.

18. Stress benefits, not features. Never assume that readers will figure out what the benefits are.

19. Always end with a call to action.

20. Test your copy in two ways:
- Read it aloud. Listen to yourself. Do you appear to be reading or having a discussion? If it sounds like reading, it is — and it needs to be reworked.
- Let someone else read it and give you feedback.

Networking

Associate yourself with men of good quality if you esteem your own reputation; for 'tis better to be alone than in bad company.

GEORGE WASHINGTON (1732–99), 1ST PRESIDENT OF THE UNITED STATES

G reat salespeople are always looking for new opportunities. Networking is one of the most effective methods to discover them. But networking successfully is both a science and an art. You can improve your chances of successfully impressing people if you do the following:

1. Network constantly. Look at every gathering as a chance to expand your network. Talk to people at your church, in the bank lineup, on the bus. Be sensitive to people who may not want to reciprocate. Back off immediately if you sense that people have little interest in pursuing the discussion.

2. Develop a 30-second conversation starter one that will allow you to
   - strike up a friendly conversation easily
   - interest people in pursuing the conversation
   - encourage people to ask you questions about what you do

3. Join committees where people of like mind and interest will be found. Volunteer for projects where there is a likelihood you will work with people who can assist you.

4. Find new places to meet people who might want your product or service. Such places include religious organizations; industry associations; self-help groups, such as Toastmasters; community service groups, such as Rotary and Kiwanis; and your chamber of commerce.

5. Work on techniques to network in a room full of strangers.
- Be the person who strikes up conversations. Find the things that you have in common with people: traffic, sports, the coffee you're drinking. Remember to be cheerful and friendly and always watch people's reactions. That way you'll know whether to change tack or keep the same approach.
- Always be ready with something witty to say, something that demonstrates your understanding without showing off.
- People are flattered and impressed when you use their names. Address people you meet by name.
- Encourage people to use your name. Wear a name tag with some conversation-starting and attention-grabbing device on it, like a happy face.
- Show a real interest in the person you're talking to and the things that she does.
- Exchange business cards. Make the other person feel good by noticing something interesting on the card. "Wow," you might say, "tell me more about that."
- Don't ask yes/no questions. Ask open-ended questions that will keep the conversation going.

- Encourage others to talk by listening patiently. Pay attention to clues about what people need or want. That way you'll be able to adapt your message to suit the person you're talking to. This will encourage others to meet your needs in return.
- Establish a bond by finding some way to be of help. Doing this will keep people interested and make them want to continue the relationship.
- The handshake is important. Shake firmly at the beginning and end of each conversation. Doing so lets the person you're talking to know that you think meeting him is important.
- Be able to explain briefly and simply what you do, and always seem enthusiastic.
- Stay upbeat and positive. Be ready with a few words to describe yourself. Are you driven? decisive? Have an interesting story ready to exemplify your description.
- Slip in an interesting detail about yourself to make the other person curious. Let people know that you are special in some way.
- Make sure you're dressed appropriately. Dress up when you're in doubt and always appear tidy and clean.
- Watch your body language. Don't betray your nervousness by fidgeting or slouching.
- Show your enthusiasm. Smile warmly. Be relaxed. You don't have to be someone you're not.
- Be sure that you don't seem to be name dropping or boasting. People respond much more warmly to the humility that comes from quiet confidence.
- Make sure that you are up-to-date with what is going on in your industry. Be ready to speak authoritatively about new ideas and how they can be implemented.

6. Don't wait for contacts to come to you and don't leave your networking to chance. Decide on a number of new contacts for each week and actively pursue them.

7. Follow up. If you offered to do something, make sure you do it.

8. Keep your new connections organized. Use your "contact file" to keep in touch, to send holiday cards and thank-you notes.

9. Last of all, if you're a "people" person, networking should be fun. Make it a game. You'll win some and you'll lose some. But if you win more than you lose, you'll meet your weekly goals and soon have an enviable network of contacts.

Friends, you and me.
You brought another friend, and then there were three.
We started our group . . . our circle of friends.
And like that circle, there is no beginning or end.

ANONYMOUS

Newsletters

Brevity is the soul of wit.

WILLIAM SHAKESPEARE (1564–1616), ENGLISH DRAMATIST, POET

*N*ewsletters are a wonderful way to add value to existing customers and create great impressions with prospective customers. Here are some tips on making the process effective:

1. Make sure that the front cover catches the reader's attention. It should be attractive and feature a large title (as much as 25 percent) on the front. The logo should make some reference to the company. The cover should also include a section detailing what the issue contains.

2. The newsletter itself should be visually appealing with lots of illustrations. Text looks best when presented in
- short, snappy articles with useful information
- a box if it is a special feature
- where appropriate an easy-to-read checklist format

The content of the text should

- use little or no jargon
- be rich with information and short on filler
- be short and to the point
- contain new information
- be upbeat and positive
- respect its readers and not talk down or lecture them
- contain tips that will enhance people's use of your product/service

3. Letters can be distributed a number of ways. The most common are as leaflets and electronically. While there is little research on whether electronic distribution gets more or less attention than written materials, bear in mind that electronic distribution

- costs little
- may be stored in a laptop ready to be digested on a plane trip or other quiet time
- can be distributed easily by the reader
- sends a message of being current with technology

4. An ideal newsletter will

- be 1–4 pages in length
- incorporate different kinds of information
- have a theme
- include articles that have lots of bullet points rather than lengthy text, especially text that runs longer than a page
- allow the reader to get one new idea in the first 30 seconds of scanning the information

Cold Calling

A wise man will make more opportunities than he finds.

FRANCIS BACON (1561–1626),
ENGLISH PHILOSOPHER, ESSAYIST, AND STATESMAN

Cold calling is probably the one aspect of selling that most salespeople don't enjoy. Yet many swear that cold calling is one of the most effective ways to build a client base. It can also pay big dividends if your timing is right.

There are three steps to setting up a successful sales meeting with someone who is unaware of the potential benefits you offer:

1. Conduct a preliminary mailing to prospects.

2. Follow up with telephone calls to schedule appointments.

3. Meet face-to-face to present and close.

SETTING UP THE CALL WITH A PRELIMINARY MAILING

Preliminary mailings can be an effective way to introduce yourself to a potential new client. The best mailings are comprised of three elements:

- a business envelope with the person's name, not just a title such as "owner" or "president"
- a tailored letter in which the information directly relates to the prospect.
- your smallest brochure.

A personal letter has the best chance of actually getting to the decision-maker's assistant and being read by the person you directed it to.

PREPARING FOR AN EFFECTIVE CALL

1. Your keys to success are to
- develop a great script
- practise before you start
- begin with low-risk prospects first

2. A great script takes time to develop. And it is never done; you should fine-tune it continuously. Your script will help you to
- avoid being tongue-tied
- be prepared
- build on what works well

3. A great script will
- grab someone's attention
- treat people with respect

- be upbeat
- suggest a value
- engage a person to participate
- lead to a next step on the road to a sale
- make frequent use of the person's name

4. Show enthusiasm by frequent use of "great" and "wonderful." At the same time, avoid making claims that border on outrageous.

5. Treat the process as a game. Know that you will win some and lose others. But each failure should be evaluated for lessons learned so that you can do better next time.

6. Take all seriousness out of your voice — talk to them as you would a neighbour over the fence.

7. Don't prejudge your prospects. Believe that they are nice people who would benefit from using your product/service, given sufficient information.

8. Fake it 'til you make it. Prospects can feel your unease and you don't want to come across as a desperate, anxiety-ridden salesperson calling.

9. Let your prospect guide you. If your prospect raises objections, don't defend your price or throw out a million reasons to buy your product. Learn specific techniques — ones that will shift the pressure back to the prospect because it was he who raised the objection in the first place.

10. Focus on the key issues. Don't get sidetracked by small issues that detract from key benefits.

MAKING THE CALL

1. Invest in a headset; it will give you freedom to be more animated.

2. Before you call, don't forget to take three deep breaths. Relax. You'll feel better, and be calm and more alert. Sit straight up in your chair. Look up at the ceiling and laugh loudly — the louder the better. These small exercises oxygenate your blood, which goes to the brain and increases alertness.

3. Find a phone position that works for you. If necessary
- lean back in your chair and put your feet up on your desk
- look up at the ceiling or out the window

4. Follow these steps as closely as possible:
- Introduce yourself. This is not a time for modesty, but neither is it a time for bragging. Saying "I'm Joe Soap, senior sales associate of Acme Break" is better than "I'm Soap, a salesman for Acme Break."
- Capture attention. You have only a few seconds to overcome emotions ranging from preoccupation with other tasks to outright anger at having to deal with yet another unsolicited salesperson. The first words you utter had better be engaging.
- Let the prospect know why you have called. The reason should be compelling and not sound scripted. If you can point to someone else suggesting you make the call, so much the

better. "Mr. Bean, your colleague Joe Fine suggested I call you as I've been able to reduce his costs by 23 percent. He felt that you would be interested, too."

- Don't ask the prospect whether he has read the information or if he has any questions about it. If he hasn't read it, these types of questions might only embarrass him.
- Refresh the prospect's memory by presenting a brief overview.
- Engage the prospect. Ask open-ended questions when necessary. These could include the following:
  - How do you handle these issues at your company?
  - What would it take to make you change suppliers?
  Never ask a closed-ended question that could lead to a "no" answer. The answers to your questions will give you information that will identify a need. *Your* need is to set up an appointment to demonstrate how his need will be met.
- Listening to the words only will be misleading. Listen to the nuances — the tone of voice, the pauses, the pitch, the strength or softness — and respond accordingly.
- Inject pauses periodically. Give the prospect opportunity to speak if she wants to.
- As soon as the prospect expresses interest by starting to ask detailed questions, begin to sell the appointment.
- Ask for the appointment by giving the prospect a choice between two days.

Educational Events

If you think education is expensive, try ignorance!

DEREK BOK, AMERICAN EDUCATOR, AS QUOTED IN
1,911 BEST THINGS ANYBODY EVER SAID

Conducting an educational event projects an image of being leading edge and adding value to clients at no cost. But everyone knows that they are there for a reason — to be exposed to a new concept or product that they might need to buy. Here are some tips to get the highest number of sales from such an event:

1. Find a new product or angle that may be different from anything potential clients might be aware of.

2. Create a mailing list of people who have the power to make decisions to buy. Such lists can come from
   - existing databases
   - local chambers of commerce
   - industry associations
   - organizations specializing in the creation of generic lists

3. Design a covering letter or e-mail that informs the readers

- why they should attend
- what you will cover
- the length of the program
- venue, dates, and time
- how to confirm their attendance
  Make it easy to register by using a toll-free number or by allowing readers to register electronically.

4. Book an attractive meeting place, one that will project an image you want to be associated with.

5. Pick a venue that is central to most people who are likely to attend.

6. Set a time that will be least invasive to the time of attendees. Often, an early breakfast meeting will allow attendees to get back to their offices and still put in a good day's work.

7. Consider having a guest speaker to add legitimacy to your presentation. The speaker could be

- a well-known expert
- an author
- a client with a proven track record of having used your product/service

8. Before the presentation, conduct a dry run in front of a critical audience. Ask them to rate the presentation from the point of view of the customer.

9. Ensure that the program is designed to provide useful information most of the time, rather than a continual sales pitch. The idea is to provide people with the kind of information that will make them open to a subsequent meeting.

10. Include a client testimonial that can demonstrate benefits. That will allow you to concentrate more on features.

11. Provide adequate take-away material to ensure that all features and benefits of your offering are covered.

12. End on a positive note. Thank people for attending. Invite those that want to stay behind for further discussions to do so. Indicate that you will follow up with attendees.

Telephone Techniques
to Speak to the Buyer

I've suffered from all the hang-ups known,
And none is as bad as the telephone.

RICHARD ARMOUR (1906–89), AMERICAN POET

Have you ever had problems contacting the right person? Played endless telephone tag? Here are some strategies to improve your chances of connecting.

1. Call early in the morning. If you call before 8 a.m., people are more likely to be available than they are late in the day.

2. Find out and use the buyer's cellphone number.

3. Ask for permission to call them at home if you can't connect during regular business hours. Some people even put their home phone number on their business cards, thereby inviting you to use it if all else fails.

4. Don't leave more than one message on a voice mail. If the phone is not answered the second time, hang up. If you leave another message, you may come across as desperate or pesty — neither of which is good.

5. If you are calling a direct line and the voice mail comes on, try pressing "0" to be put through to a receptionist or assistant. Ask the person if he would be kind enough to find your party. Or, ask if there is a good time to call.

6. You may be told that the person is in a meeting. Ask whether the meeting is with a staff member or an outsider. If it is with a staff member, ask the person if they can be interrupted.

7. If you reach a receptionist after dialling "0," ask if she would mind trying to track your party down, or page them, or both. If she agrees, ask for her name and thank her.

8. Send an e-mail to your potential buyer and ask for a time when you can call.

9. Rely more on e-mail. You will get a response more often than not, even if it takes a day or two.

Referrals

A large number of acquaintances is like an orchard
full of fruit waiting to be picked.

UNKNOWN

*Y*our sales strategy can increase sales by 25 percent if you leverage the people who know and trust you. It's simply the fastest way to improve your credibility and increase sales.

1. Referral selling has several advantages, include these:
- You win instant trust. A referral from a credible source will immediately reduce the prospect's apprehension of dealing with someone new.
- You expand your network of people, all of whom are potential clients.
- You reduce your cost of sales. Opening new accounts is extremely costly and time-consuming. It costs five times more to open an account "cold" than it does to get business from an existing client.
- You make the person who gave you the referral look good, particularly if he is delighted with the service you have provided.

2. There are two ways to get referrals:

- Do great work, prompting your customers to brag about your product or service to others.
- Ask for a referral.

3. Seek referrals from the following:

- *Delighted customers.* Maintaining strong relationships with people can bring huge dividends in the form of appropriate leads.
- *Friends.* Your closest friends will know of your abilities and will want to assist you.
- *Potential customers.* Often during a sales interview, a potential client might show some resistance from a money or timing point of view, even though they are praising your product. This gives you a wonderful opportunity to ask them who might value the product more immediately.
- *Family.* Most of us have an aversion to mixing family and business. But those in your family that express an interest in helping you are likely to provide solid leads and have no need for any special thanks.
- *Vendors.* Your suppliers value your relationship and business. They have a vested interest in being helpful. Why not take advantage and tap them for appropriate referrals?

4. When should you ask for a referral? A good time is when

- you have recently completed some task that has particularly pleased the client
- your product/service is working really well
- the customer has made a major commitment to you

5. Asking for a referral is not always easy. So make it count! Don't phrase your question in a way that invites a "no." Ask "Who else do you know that would benefit from this service?"

6. Most satisfied clients will help you, but they differ in how they want to do it. They may
   - prefer to make the contact themselves
   - want little involvement in the contact
   - dictate specifically how you are to initiate the contact

7. Asking for a referral should include
   - who the ideal prospect is
   - what you can offer that prospect
   - how you propose to contact the prospect

8. If you are offered a referral, learn as much about the prospect as possible so as to enhance your possibility of success. Find out
   - her name, organization, address, phone/fax/e-mail number(s)
   - why she was chosen
   - how she could benefit from your service

9. Ask your contact if you can mention him by name.

10. People complain about disappointments to others more often than they rave about positive experiences. When they do talk about great experiences it is because
   - they like to help others
   - they can show how smart they were in selecting the service
   - they're doing a "favour" that can be called upon later in another context

11. Send a thank-you letter or make a call to the person who
provided the referral. Let them know that you

- made the contact
- may be able to serve the prospect effectively
- appreciate the referral

12. Consider thanking the person even more for a successful
outcome.

- Give them something personal. It's not a question of how
  much you spend, but rather whether the item is meaningful.
- Give them something that they would want to show others.

13. Decide on the best method of making contact: in writing, by
phone, or both. Strong referrals should probably be acted upon
quickly by phone. A letter followed by a phone call might be
better for a lukewarm prospect.

14. Organize a three-way meeting if possible. Your satisfied customer
can do the selling and you can close!

15. Make the call soon. The longer you wait, the lower the probability
of success. Your satisfied customer's enthusiasm for helping you
will surely wane with time

16. Prepare for your call by reviewing the client profile. Find out about

- the nature of their business
- recent developments in their industry
- their personality profile, family, likes and dislikes
- a key hot button
- the best way to begin the conversation to gain their attention

17. Start the call by stating who you are and who suggested you call and why.

18. Wait for a response. Then, unless the response is strongly negative, describe in general terms how clients have benefited from your product/service.

19. Ask open-ended questions about the potential client's needs.

20. State your motivation to call in terms of fulfilling an obligation, rather wanting a sale. Say, "Sam Smith asked me to call you and I promised I would."

Speaking at
Conferences

*I do not object to people looking at their watches
when I am speaking. But I strongly object when they start
shaking them to make sure they are still going.*

WILLIAM NORMAN BIRKETT (1883–1962), BRITISH LAWYER

*N*ever pass up an opportunity to impress others, particularly if you can have a captive audience. But make sure you impress the audience with your brilliance and charisma.

One doesn't often get the opportunity to present ideas in front of an audience, at a trade show or conference. It is imperative that you don't blow the opportunity by boring or confusing the audience.

PREPARING

Good presentations stand out because they follow the audience's logical thought process. To create the most effective presentation, prepare yourself by asking the following questions:

1. Who is the audience? What levels are they at in the organization? What are their needs and expectations? What will galvanize them to action and what are the triggers that will turn them off like a light bulb? What have they heard lately? How did they receive previous information?

2. What is the objective? What is the desired outcome of the presentation? Is it to provide information about a new product/service? Is it to conduct a public relations exercise and create a favourable impression?

3. How will the audience benefit? This question is important since, without benefits, the audience might lose interest quickly. Will the audience be better able to use your product/service? Will they be able to save time, or money?

4. Can you justify the benefits? Do you have any studies that prove the benefits you are recommending? Have you testimonials that support your conclusion?

5. What are your credentials? You will not want to bore the audience by bragging about your accomplishments in the area you will be speaking about, but you will want to be introduced by someone in a manner that leaves the audience in no doubt that you are the big kahuna!

6. Do you have analogies? It is useful to give examples of how your product works or benefits the audience in everyday terms and examples.

7. Do you have a case study? Can you show an example of how an organization similar to that of the audience has benefited from your product/service? Can you back up the success with data, leaving no one in doubt as to the value of your information?

PRESENTING YOUR INFORMATION

1. Create a good impression by the value of the information you are giving. The better you are, the more people will be inclined to approach you for a business card afterwards.

2. Provide a handout summarizing your key points. Attach your business card or a brochure to the handout.

3. Don't speak theoretically. Tell stories and give real-life examples. Your audience will not only find this more interesting, they'll stay awake and listen!

4. Never sell your product or service directly. Allow your examples and case studies to prove your point. Allow the introducer to extol your virtues.

5. Let people know how they can contact you. Have lots of business cards and brochures available.

6. If you can get a list of attendees, send them a follow-up letter detailing how you can help them. Include a postpaid card, phone number, and e-mail address to give them options as to how to contact you.

7. If you cannot get a list of attendees, consider getting as many business cards as possible by offering one or two prizes to people who enter a draw by dropping their business cards in a box.

8. If people approach you for a business card, ask them for theirs. This way you have more control when it comes to making contact.

Trade Shows:

Planning for Success

*Our greatest glory consists not in never failing,
but in rising every time we fall.*

RALPH WALDO EMERSON (1803–82), AMERICAN POET AND ESSAYIST

*W*hether you're attending or exhibiting at a trade show, networking opportunities abound. According to the Centre for Exhibit Industry Research, it costs 62 percent less to close a lead generated from a show than one that originated in the field. Yet most exhibitors sit behind a table, snacking and visiting with co-workers.

With proper planning, you can turn a trade show experience into a business-building bonanza. Here are the strategies to help you make the most of opportunities at trade shows:

1. Select a trade show that will attract the greatest number of potential buyers. The easiest type of show to prospect is one where potential customers are themselves exhibiting. They make it easy for you to know where to find them. They have a whole booth filled with information about themselves, their products and services. But even when your targets are attendees, it's still possible to do some successful targeting.

2. Set goals for what you want to achieve at the show. You might think in terms of the number of

- new prospects
- samples you want to distribute
- people who will test your product
- follow-up appointments
- sales

3. Create a plan.

- *Define* your ideal prospect profile. Set up appointments before you arrive. Review the attendee list, and see who's there that you want to meet for the first time.
- *Decide* whom you want to meet. Go beyond the initial criteria to include visitors from companies who outsource services in your category and have a current need.
- *Decide* what you're looking for before you head to the trade show, and take the time to train your team to pursue only those prospects who fit your profile.
- *Consider* the best way to meet prospects. Can you, for example, have people find you because you are a speaker?
- *Identify* which booths you want to see. Study the exhibit layout and map so you don't waste time and energy.

4. Offer your services as a speaker. You will gain much free publicity by presenting yourself as a fountain of knowledge. Capitalize on the opportunity by

- informing your prospects and customers that you are a featured speaker and therefore an expert
- inviting them to hear you speak
- sending them a list of the ideas you presented, once the show

is over, and letting all your customers know how your presentation went

5. Offer to write an article for the show's Web site or magazine. Try to have your picture printed with the article to encourage greater recognition. Be sure your contact information is included. If the show has a Web site, ask to be listed.

6. Send a press release. Contact media in the host town about your hot new ideas. You could be interviewed in the paper, on TV, or on the radio. Have a toll-free phone number for people to order products or to get a free sample. You could offer a tip sheet on the top 10 ways to use your kind of service or "The 10 Myths of . . ."

7. Volunteer to introduce a speaker or panel. This is a great opportunity because you don't have to prepare much, you have visibility and credibility, and your name could be in the program.

8. If you don't have the funds for a booth on your own, consider sharing space. If there is an exhibitor at the show who sells to the same kinds of prospects as you, but who is not a competitor, ask whether you can pay a modest fee (say $50 or $100) to set up a rack of your brochures in their booth.

9. Arrange as many appointments as you can in advance. Send a personalized invitation to prospects. Find a way to express, in as few words as possible, why customers should take time to meet you. For example, offer them
- a "show special" or advance news of an exciting product development
- new solutions to some of their concerns

- a new state-of-the-art system
- a cost-cutting device

10. Follow up with a call to set up a meeting. Remember, many people would rather "float" at the show and not be tied down. Secure in advance the appointments you're able to, and when you get to the show, immediately work on getting more.

11. Meet with existing customers, too. Some will expect you to give them special attention. Each category will require specific preparation on your part. Give attendees a reason to make meeting you a top priority.

12. Track down potential customers who are not exhibiting. They go to shows to see the exhibits and attend the sessions. Your best way to meet these people is through the seminar and presentation sessions. Take a look at the trade show agenda and try to determine the most popular sessions. Plan to attend them yourself.

13. Many shows help you to identify potential buyers by having different colour tags for exhibitors, press, buyers, etc. Watching out for these will help you zero in on your target group.

14. Collect business cards of potential customers by offering a draw. People who submit their cards know that they will be contacted, so you're assured of a reasonable return by following up with these people. Many shows rent hand-held card scanners, which allow you to quickly scan people's business cards and download them daily onto your computer. Using such a scanner will allow you more time to focus on making as many contacts as possible instead of spending time on data entry activities.

15. Spend an extra day or two meeting other contacts in the city you have travelled to. Make them feel as if you are coming into town especially to see them. This is a great way to leverage the time and cost of the show.

Trade Shows:

Maximizing the Opportunity

If opportunity doesn't knock, build a door.

MILTON BERLE, AMERICAN COMEDIAN

A good way to find new prospects is to exhibit at trade shows. You have a booth where people come to find out more about what you do. You talk to prospects and you hand out literature. But what if you don't have the financial and other resources to be an exhibitor? Can you still use a trade show to develop good sales leads? The answer, of course, is yes. Here are some tips for prospecting at trade shows:

IF YOU ARE A NON-EXHIBITOR

1. Take the opportunity not only to network but educate yourself about the newest developments and trends. Here are three ways to accomplish this.
   - Carry a small tape recorder. Record things you want to remember to do or the names of people to see. Capture new ideas. Adapt ideas from other industries.
   - Ask interesting exhibitors lots of questions. Look at the

brochures and ask the exhibitors to clarify anything you
don't understand. Take or record notes.
- Spread out your resources. Don't roam the room with your
co-workers.

2. If you're not exhibiting, have an advertising specialty to give
away. People may throw out brochures and papers from booths,
but they rarely throw out an advertising specialty (other than one
more pen or key chain). Learn from those who attend as well as
from those who exhibit.

3. Ask the exhibitor the name of the person you should contact for
your specific goals. Write that name on the exhibitor's card. Ask
if you can use the exhibitor's name when calling your contact
person (so you won't be making a cold call).

4. Network at every opportunity.
- Talk to people who wander from booth to booth. Find out their
interests. What draws them in?
- Use the buffet as a networking venue, not as if it were your last
meal. It's hard to speak with a full mouth. It's hard to shake
hands while you balance a plate and a glass. And it's hard to
exchange cards when you've got dip-covered fingers. Try not to
carry more than one thing from a buffet table. It will give you
a free hand to help someone else — a great way to start a
conversation and introduce yourself.
- Attend educational sessions with the people you want to meet.
Introduce yourself, talk, and share your learning experience.
Now you have something in common. You've already begun a
relationship. Visit before the seminar. Ask for the cards of the
people sitting on each side of you. Turn around. Who is sitting

behind you? Who is in front of you? If you decide to respond to a question or ask a question, say your name, company and/or what you do when you respond. For instance: "I'm Karen Susman, national speaker, trainer and coach, and I'd like to ask . . ."

5. Rest. Freshen up often. Your discomfort and pain can show on your face.

6. Stay organized. Discard unnecessary materials at the end of each day.

7. Evaluate the best prospects at the end of each day. Use this approach:
   - Using the floor plan in the show literature, go back over your tour, booth by booth. Think about each of the people you met, the companies they represent, and how likely they are to be a prospect for your products and services.
   - Create "A," "B," and "C" lists for prospects. Put the hottest prospects into the "A" list, moderate prospects into the "B" list, and the rest into the "C" list.

8. Develop a battle plan to turn contacts into selling appointments. For your hottest prospects, make a note on
   - what you know about them
   - how you might best start a conversation with them
   - what you could say that would be of interest or importance to them
   - who the key decision-makers are
   - how you might get to the decision-makers
   - when the best (quietest) time to approach each prospect is

9. Implement your plan. Start by practising your strategy on a few of your "B" list potential clients. When you feel comfortable with your approach, turn your attention to the "A" list.

10. Remember, the people you are approaching are there to sell, not to buy. So don't expect people to spend much time with you at the show. You are doing well if you have
- introduced yourself
- confirmed their agreement to meet you later
- taken their business card

11. Send postcards from the show site to key people in your network. Tell them you've got some great new ideas for them. Follow up when you return home.

12. Follow up immediately with important contacts. Even a brief note will remind them of you and your company. Handwritten notes are so unusual that the recipient will be impressed. If someone requests information, get right on it.

IF YOU ARE AN EXHIBITOR

1. Be proactive. If you're working the show, don't stay behind the table. Ask visitors about their businesses so you can show them appropriate products or information. This means you must listen attentively. Don't sell your product or service; sell what the product will do for your visitors.

2. Sponsor an award or contest. This could be a draw or an award for guessing the number of brochures you brought to the trade show. Or sponsor a contest for the most creative way your services can be used. How about sponsoring an award for industry person or emerging leader of the year? Doing so will give you national recognition.

3. Be ready with "case histories" of your successes. Help visitors by painting a picture of how they could use your products: "Just imagine . . ."

4. Talk to as many people as possible so that you can qualify them. The trade show isn't the time for small talk. If they meet your initial criteria, take the conversation to the next step and probe further to determine if your ideal prospect profile is achieved.

5. Leave literature in a public place. Nearly all shows have literature tables out front. At the top shows, these are strictly reserved for paid exhibitors and regularly policed to remove non-exhibitor materials. At most local shows, however, the rules are looser or are not enforced. At these, consider leaving a few copies of your brochure on the table, and return a few times a day to make sure your pile is neat and visible.

6. Invite clients that have had success with your product or service to be part of your exhibit. There is nothing so powerful as a personal endorsement. Offer them something tangible in return.

7. Keep your booth neat and clean at all times to make it as inviting as possible.

8. Avoid having too many salespeople on duty at the same time for fear of intimidating buyers. Leave open spaces for people to wander in and get comfortable in your space.

9. Project a relaxed atmosphere to encourage people to visit and open themselves up to your conversation.

10. Be aware of different greeting practices of other cultures, particularly if the show you're exhibiting at attracts an international audience.

IF YOU ARE A SPEAKER, OR ON A PANEL

1. Get to know the other panelists before your presentation. This will make for a better presentation, and you'll be networking and building relationships with other movers and shakers. Keep in touch afterward.

2. During the formal presentation, take good notes on areas that apply to your selling. Before and after the presentation, talk to as many of the people around you as you can, and collect business cards.

Trade Shows:

When the Show Is Over

Let deeds follow words now.

LECH WALESA, POLISH LABOUR ACTIVIST, POLITICIAN

Trade shows work, but only if you follow up. Your goal at any trade show is to get sales, not visitors. Trade shows aren't the end of the sales process, they're just a key part. To get sales, you need a follow-up system designed to build relationships and nurture them through the buying cycle.

1. After the show, follow up with each of the people you met at these sessions. Depending on the number, use a letter or phone call to make contact. Use the content of the presentation or something you spoke about with them as the focus of your conversation, finishing up with some question you would like to explore further the next time you talk. That conversation is, of course, your first appointment.

2. If some of your prospects were show exhibitors, remember that they will be very busy right after the show sending out literature and following up on their own hot leads. Consider waiting a week to 10 days before contacting them.

3. Build an integrated response management program. Start with your "A" list first and decide, based on your knowledge of each person, how best to approach them. Never leave multiple messages. The more messages you leave, the more desperate you may appear to be. If phone calls are your chosen method of communication, call till they pick up the phone. If you are getting frustrated, consider
   - having an assistant track them down for you
   - sending them a card asking for a time to call
   - using e-mail
   - calling at an unusual hour

4. If you do make contact on the phone, identify yourself and the name of your company and your past history with the individual.

5. Go slowly with your introduction, breaking it into separate sentences. Remember, the prospect is still concentrating on something else. Give her a chance to hear you and understand what you are saying.

6. Tell the prospect why you are calling — to follow up on the mailing you sent.

7. Inject pauses. Give the prospect an opportunity to speak if he wants to.

8. Don't ask the prospect whether she has read the information or has any questions about it.

9. Refresh the prospect's memory by presenting a brief overview of

your company. Personalize this as much as possible by
mentioning information you have about his company.

10. As soon as the prospect expresses interest by starting to ask
detailed questions, begin to sell the appointment. In order to
answer the prospect's questions, you need to know more about
her business.

11. Ask for an appointment by giving the prospect a choice between
two days. The prospect will likely pick one or come up with a date
and time of his own. Do not ask, "When is a good time for you?"
Most business owners are too busy to have a "good" time.

12. Throughout the conversation, always listen to the prospect
without interruption. The more she says to you, the more she
becomes involved in considering the purchase.

Samples

The proof of the pudding is in the eating.
By a small sample we may judge of the whole piece.

MIGUEL DE CERVANTES (1547–1616),
SPANISH NOVELIST, DRAMATIST, AND POET

Giving potential clients a sample will enable them to try your product/service at no risk to themselves. Moreover, it will demonstrate your confidence in your offering. Finally, it will make them obligated to at least give you feedback, or at most to give you an order.

1. Samples are used extensively in the food and pharmaceutical industries. They might also come in these forms:
   - free attendance at a workshop for one person in a large company
   - a free meal in anticipation of booking a banquet
   - a vehicle test drive
   - tasting of products in supermarkets
   - a free sample of a household product, including food, personal toiletries, or household cleaning products

2. Key principles in providing samples are these:
- Give only enough to enable a potential client to evaluate the product/service.
- Provide the samples to the most likely buyers.

3. People may be tempted to buy your product but their interest will decline the longer you wait to contact them. So make contact early and ask them
- to provide feedback
- to buy, using an open-ended question, such as
  - "What else do I need to do to get the green light?"
  - "What other information do you need before we proceed?"

4. If your feedback was enthusiastic, consider an even more assertive and direct approach. For example:
- "When could we start?"
- "Which is the best delivery time for you?"

The Selling Process

2

A Step-by-Step
Approach

*There is no sudden leap into the stratosphere. There is only advancing
step by step . . . up the pyramid towards your goals.*

BEN STEIN, AMERICAN ACTOR

*S*elling is an art. But it is also a science in that success is much higher
if a systematic, step-by-step process is followed. These are the steps:

Step 1: Opening
Step 2: Exploring and confirming the customer's needs
Step 3: Presenting your solutions
Step 4: Dealing with objections
Step 5: Closing

We will describe each step before going into more detail in subsequent
chapters.

Step 1: OPENING

1. The opening takes place on the phone or in person. Either way,
your task is to make a great impression by presenting yourself
in a relaxed, friendly manner.

2. Your non-verbal communications should reinforce the verbal messages. The potential buyer will be judging the way you walk, your dress, posture, and facial expressions.

3. In your first few moments, you should do the following:
   - Greet the customer, telling her who you are and who you work for.
   - Explain the purpose of your visit. Give a precise picture of your goal for the meeting, in 15 words or less.
   - Inform the customer of the benefits to be gained from the meeting.
   - Confirm that the customer is willing to collaborate with you (or deal with their reluctance if not).

Step 2: EXPLORING AND CONFIRMING THE CUSTOMER'S NEEDS

1. With an agreement to pursue your discussion, you now need to
   - develop trust
   - establish your competence
   - establish the needs of the customer

2. Find out what needs the customer may have by probing for information. Open-ended questions will demonstrate your interest, particularly if you make notes, confirm your understanding, and summarize from time to time.

Step 3: PRESENTING YOUR SOLUTIONS

1. With a complete understanding of the needs of the customer, you are now in a position to present your solutions. You will present both features and benefits.

2. Features are the characteristics of the product or service, such as
   - the nature of the product
   - the way it works
   - its purpose
   - its physical characteristics

3. Benefits describe the satisfaction the customer will derive from your offering. A benefit is most effective when you relate it to a need that the customer has described and provide proof that the benefit will be secured.

Step 4: DEALING WITH OBJECTIONS

1. At this stage you are looking for signs of interest, dealing with concerns and generating commitment.

2. Objections are good. They give you insight into the concerns of the customer, and once you remove the roadblocks, you will legitimately be able to close. In overcoming objections, you must
   - acknowledge the buyer's concern
   - probe to make sure that you fully understand
   - respond to the concern
   - confirm that you have dealt satisfactorily with the concern

Step 5: CLOSING

1. Closing the sale is a natural outcome of handling the previous four steps effectively.

2. Closing the sale is best done if you
- summarize key points, focusing on benefits
- ask for a commitment

3. If the response is positive, nail down the details of the sale such as specifications and delivery. If you get a negative response, go back to Step 4 and deal with any remaining objections before attempting to close again.

First Impressions

First impressions are the most lasting.

TRADITIONAL PROVERB

The first few minutes of a meeting will either endear you to a potential buyer or turn him off. Your chances of impressing him can be increased dramatically if you keep the following principles in mind:

1. Be conscious of your body language.
  - Shake hands firmly — but don't break any bones! A caution though: not all cultures shake hands, let alone firmly. Be conscious of who you are dealing with. Generally the more prolonged the handshake, the stronger the signal that you have been accepted.
  - Maintain eye contact. Focus on the person's eyes without staring.
  - Smile warmly. Show your genuine happiness at meeting the person with a broad, relaxed smile.

2. You'll know that your greeting has not been accepted the person does any of the following:

- leans away from you
- looks puzzled
- fails to smile
- crosses arms
- fidgets with hands
- fails to reciprocate with a firm handshake
- sits with legs crossed and moves away from you

3. If your first approach did not work, consider Plan B. You should
  - not begin to present ideas until you know there is interest in hearing what you have to say/show
  - ask open-ended questions to get them more involved and give you clues as to the reason for their lack of enthusiasm
  - listen to what they are saying — verbally and non-verbally
  - maintain your positive and enthusiastic approach — albeit somewhat toned down
  - behave as if you have been accepted so as not to show disappointment in any way

4. Dress appropriately. Dress codes differ widely depending on
  - the industry
  - the rank of the individual within the organization
  - the part of the country you are in
  - whether your customer is in a rural or urban area
  - the size of the organization
  - the age of the person you are visiting

  For example:
  - People in the high-tech industry would probably feel comfortable meeting someone dressed in business casual.
  - If in doubt, dress conservatively. For example, a man from the

Middle East might not take seriously a saleswoman wearing
an above-the-knee skirt.

- Some situations call for you to dress down. For example, a
farmer might feel alienated by a salesman in a three-piece suit.

5. In summary, first impressions are best made when you
- smile warmly
- greet people with a firm handshake
- look people in the eye
- show interest in them as people, not just as prospects
- dress similarly to them, or perhaps one notch more formal,
but never more casual
- wear clean, pressed clothes
- are properly groomed
- do not reek of cologne
- look the part

The Top 10 Turn-ons

Customers are desperately looking for someone to be loyal to; a trusted and respected partner. Be that partner!

KEN IMRIE, SALES COACH, IBM CANADA

Here is a list of attributes that will ensure your career in sales is successful and rewarding:

1. **Credibility.** This is the ability to consistently demonstrate
  - a willingness to listen
  - enthusiasm to go the extra mile
  - commitment to complete what you undertake

2. **Knowledge.** Have accurate answers about your
  - industry
  - company
  - products
  - delivery capability
  - competitors' products/services/strengths and weaknesses

If you don't know, get as much information as possible and follow up with the answers. Ask questions that demonstrate interest and caring. Fully understand your client's business and needs before sharing how you can help. Always keep your client up-to-date on the latest trends in their field. Send them notes and articles and invite them to seminars that will make them more knowledgeable.

3. **Speed.** Getting things done quickly will win you accolades galore. With communications capable of being sent around the world in seconds or milliseconds, and the availability of devices to stay constantly in touch, there is no excuse for tardiness. As a rule
- return calls within two hours
- return e-mails daily
- process orders daily

4. **Reliability.** A true professional always delivers. Always meet your commitments or let people know well ahead of time if you may not be able to.

5. **Attitude.** Always think positively. See the glass as half full rather than half empty. Positive people are like magnets — they attract other positive people. Negative people, of course, do likewise. Thinking good thoughts will also make you feel good. And when you feel good, you perform well.

6. **Empathy.** Show that you care. Listen 80 percent of the time and speak only 20 percent.

7. **Humanity.** Get to know your clients as people. Learn to treat them as friends. Behave as a friend. Lean towards an informal relationship based on mutual help and trust.

8. **Under-promising and over-delivering.** Surprise your clients with unexpected levels of service and caring that will knock their socks off! Have them become your best advocates. Let them share news of your remarkable service to other potential clients.

9. **Professionalism.** Being friendly will never interfere with professionalism. Always keep promises, return communications quickly, avoid getting involved in the politics of the client organization, and avoid any sexist, racist, homophobic, or ethnic jokes.

10. **Demonstrated caring.** Follow up to make sure expectations have been met. And call before bad news might reach the client — before they call you!

The Top 10 Turnoffs

Artificial intelligence is no match for natural stupidity.

UNKNOWN

*H*ere is a list of things which, if done regularly, will ensure that your career in sales is short lived:

1. **Inappropriate attire.** Always dress smartly and neatly. Never dress to stand out or be so different from your potential buyer that your appearance distracts. Avoid
   - overuse of jewelry
   - provocative (revealing) clothing

2. **Exaggeration.** Certainly, you want to be enthusiastic about your product, service, and company. But buyers are not stupid. They can tell the difference between fantasy and truth. Comments such as "We never have returns" can be better said as "We have only a 2 percent return rate." And "We are the best by far" can be better put as "A.C. Neilsen ranks us among the top 2 percent in our industry."

3. **Pressure tactics.** Pushing for a sale is a sign of desperation. It suggests that you
- are ignoring the needs of the potential buyer and are focusing purely on your own needs
- have no empathy for the situation of the potential buyer
- are putting up a smoke screen to cover weaknesses in your offering

4. **Inattentiveness.** Talking incessantly is a sure way to lose customers, because you're not learning what their needs are. And trying to sell something that has no value to a potential buyer is arrogant. Either find something that the customer needs or find a customer who has a need compatible with what you have to offer.

5. **Harassment.** People hate being hounded mercilessly. They feel like they are being boxed into a corner. If you are able to get a sale in the short term, you will find that it may be of nominal value, just to get rid of you. And you will then find that a significant-sized sale will be that much more elusive.

6. **Going over the buyer's head.** As difficult as it may be to get a sale from a buyer, it can be a death knell to go over her head to complain. Embarrassing someone will produce resentment and a permanent cold shoulder.

7. **Unreliability.** Keep all your promises. Follow through on all your commitments.

8. **Too much information.** Dumping is the process of listing all the features of your offering to the client before you are aware of their needs. This is a major turnoff. Selling is the art of defining needs by probing for information through questioning and listening.

9. **Arrogance.** Success sometimes goes to one's head. When it does, it expresses itself in overconfidence, boasting, and exaggeration. Arrogance is insufferable, and will soon lead to strained relations and loss of business.

10. **Any combination of the above!!**

3
Getting on the
Customer's Wavelength

Reading Body Language

Silence is one great art of conversation.

WILLIAM HAZLITT (1778–1830), ENGLISH WRITER

Salespeople must be tuned in to the needs of customers. These needs are often hard to understand, as the client does not verbalize them. One has to become expert in "reading" people though their gestures and other non-verbal cues.

Albert Mehrabian's studies on communication concluded that communication can be broken down to 55 percent non-verbal, 38 percent vocal, and 7 percent verbal.

As different cultures have different ways of expressing themselves non-verbally, one should not jump quickly to conclusions. In Western society, however, the following are generally accepted cues to determine the thoughts and feelings of the person you are communicating with.

Non-verbal thoughts can be put into three categories: acceptance, caution, and disapproval. Here are the primary indicators of each:

1. Acceptance is probable if the person
   - leans forward or sits upright

- begins smiling, takes renewed interest
- takes hold of your product or tightens his grip if you are trying to retrieve it
- relaxes his arms and has open palms
- crosses his legs and points them towards you
- uncrosses his legs

2. Caution and doubt may be surfacing if the person
   - looks away from you
   - crosses her legs and points them away from you
   - looks away from you
   - looks upward and to the right
   - begins to fidget with something
   - crosses her arms

3. Disapproval is evident if the person
   - physically moves away from you
   - shows anger
   - wrinkles his face and brow
   - becomes silent
   - avoids looking at you
   - crosses his arms
   - clenches his fist or gestures to show rejection
   - crosses his legs and swivels his body away from you

Here is how to interpret and respond to various types of body language:
- *Crossed legs and arms.* It could mean that the person is defensive and not open to your ideas. Ask an open-ended question to find out what's on his mind.
- *Darting eyes.* She is probably anxious or lacks confidence. Help her feel secure.

- *Blank stares.* The person is probably not listening to you. Ask a question to get him to refocus. If he has no idea what you're talking about, consider summarizing your thoughts.
- *Looking up at top left.* Watch out! She is probably figuring out how to outmanoeuvre you. She may even be lying. Ask for evidence of any comment made.
- *Looking up at top right.* He may be thinking about something, but unable at the time to fully grasp the situation. Consider waiting for a while until he focuses back on you.
- *Hands on hip or has a hip jut.* The person is displaying confidence, and possibly arrogance. Don't pick an argument, but look for areas of common agreement.
- *Hands at side.* This neutral posture requires little adjustment in your communications.
- *Arms crossed.* This could indicate a closed attitude. Through probing questions, try to determine what roadblocks are in the way of your progress.
- *Jacket buttoned up.* This may indicate a need to be formal. Conduct the discussion without being personal.
- *Jacket unbuttoned.* The person is informal and open. This will allow you to proceed more quickly than would be the case otherwise. Assume that the person is onside and proceed as if the sale has been accepted even without verbal confirmation.
- *Leaning forward.* She is interested in what you are saying. Close earlier rather than later.
- *Leaning back with arms behind head.* The person is contemplating your words and is possibly sceptical. Through open-ended questions, find out what reservations he may have and deal with them.
- *Looking over bifocals.* The person is being judgemental and sceptical. Don't challenge her, but ask questions that might

help you understand her thinking at this point. "What are your thoughts?" or "How do you feel about this?" could be appropriate questions.

- *Hands open with palms down.* This might indicate a demanding gesture. Be prepared to disarm him by being helpful and courteous. Don't fight back. Try to remove his hostility.
- *Open hand with palms up.* This may signal that she has a need. Offer help.
- *Hands on the table.* This could signal a willingness to get things done. Try to close sooner rather than later.
- *Sitting in a slouched position.* This may indicate a lack of confidence and self-esteem. Find something positive to say that might make the person feel more important.
- *Blinking slowly.* This might suggest that he is not feeling good about being in the meeting. Try to confirm that this might be the case and do something that will reward his presence.
- *Smiling.* The person is enjoying the discussion. Good! Proceed towards the goal you have set for the discussion.
- *Head angled downward.* He is embarrassed, shy, or possibly lying. If you believe that the response is due to some lack of confidence, pass a compliment that may be appropriate to the situation, avoiding any patronizing comments. If you feel that the person is lying, ask him for evidence of his opinion. Or, show him evidence that his opinion is incorrect. Focus at all times on the issue rather than the person.
- *Head tilted back.* This may indicate arrogance. Don't respond to her superiority, or become distracted by it. Rather, focus on the issue at hand.
- *Head cocked to the side.* He is probably deeply interested in what you are saying. Keep talking, focusing on benefits. Look for an opportunity to close.

In using body language, try always to show a positive, open approach to encourage reciprocity. The best combination might be

- leaning slightly forward
- cocking your head slightly to the side
- keeping your arms at your side
- smiling

Any negative change in body language should provoke you into action.

- Ask them if their sentiments have changed, and if so, why?
- Move away from your formal presentation to re-establish a connection.
- Listen carefully to objections and deal with them fully before moving on.
- Maintain your sense of confidence and enthusiasm.

Listening

The best approach to customer-focused selling is asking good questions, then listening intently to the answers. Selling is not about talking well; it's the ability to gather information, consolidate the information and provide helpful intervention (your product or service).

MARGUERITE SMOLEN, *THE EVERYTHING SELLING BOOK*

Selling is about meeting needs. The closer you can match what you have to offer with the needs of the buyer, the greater the probability of a sale. The best way to know the true needs of the buyer is to listen to her. Listening will enable you to gain valuable knowledge that you can apply in matching your product/service to the buyer's needs. Listening also helps to identify problems, issues, concerns, and opportunities. It would be a pure fluke to sell something without knowing what your customer really wants. Here are some invaluable tips to improve your listening:

1. Listening will show the potential buyer that she is *understood.* She will sense your desire to help her. So, give her your undivided attention. Don't do other work or take calls while you are listening.

2. Your attention is what makes a conversation succeed or fail. Don't answer your telephone or appear distracted by other work if you are supposed to be listening.

3. Meet in a quiet place if possible. A noisy or busy public place will only distract you both.

4. Don't waste your time and energy working on a rebuttal. Listen carefully and allow yourself to be swayed.

5. Don't interrupt. You should only cut in if it seems the other person is repeating herself to clarify a point that you already understand.

6. Let the other person know you're interested. Nod from time to time and say "aha" or something similar.

7. Look the other person in the eye without appearing rude or aggressive.

8. Use your body language to communicate. Lean forward to show you're interested. Smile. Don't fidget or let your eyes wander.

9. Don't be embarrassed to ask for clarification. Summarize what the other person is saying from time to time: "So what you're saying is . . ."

10. Don't finish the speaker's sentences. This shows impatience.

11. Don't interrupt even though the person might have difficulty making a point. Let others finish before you confirm your understanding. Train yourself to slowly count to five before interjecting or saying something.

12. Learn to let short, comfortable silences descend on a conversation. A moment of quiet will encourage the other person to speak.

13. Give the other person the opportunity to say what he means by asking open-ended questions. For example: "What else can you tell me about that?"

14. If the answers you get are long and complex, ask the client for permission to make notes. Alternatively, echo back to them your understanding to show that you have truly understood. Say, "So what I'm hearing you say is . . . Have I got that right?"

15. Keep your eyes open for clues about what the person is really thinking. Body language can tell you a great deal more than the messages you hear.

It's so simple to be wise.
Just think of something stupid to say and then don't say it.

SAM LEVINSON, POPULAR COMEDIAN

A Listening Self-Test

Answer the following questions quickly and honestly.

Choose **1** if you disagree totally
2 if you disagree somewhat
3 if you neither agree or disagree
4 if you agree somewhat
5 if you agree totally

When meeting with clients/potential clients, I

1.	do most of the talking	**1**	**2**	**3**	**4**	**5**
2.	tend to interrupt often	**1**	**2**	**3**	**4**	**5**
3.	tend to develop rebuttals instead of listening	**1**	**2**	**3**	**4**	**5**
4.	tend to be argumentative	**1**	**2**	**3**	**4**	**5**
5.	get frustrated if they don't see my point of view	**1**	**2**	**3**	**4**	**5**
6.	tend to finish people's sentences	**1**	**2**	**3**	**4**	**5**
7.	change the subject if I feel I'm getting nowhere	**1**	**2**	**3**	**4**	**5**
8.	ignore body language	**1**	**2**	**3**	**4**	**5**
9.	feel uncomfortable maintaining eye contact	**1**	**2**	**3**	**4**	**5**

10. see things from my point of view rather than the customers'	**1**	**2**	**3**	**4**	**5**
11. pretend to understand when I don't	**1**	**2**	**3**	**4**	**5**
12. think about what I'm going to say rather than what is being said	**1**	**2**	**3**	**4**	**5**
13. ignore changes in body language of the client	**1**	**2**	**3**	**4**	**5**
14. listen intently, but fail to recognize what the person is feeling	**1**	**2**	**3**	**4**	**5**
15. fail to grasp emotionally laden words	**1**	**2**	**3**	**4**	**5**
16. never listen to the meaning behind the words	**1**	**2**	**3**	**4**	**5**
17. fail to see things from the other person's perspective	**1**	**2**	**3**	**4**	**5**
18. neglect to start conversations with a conscious attitude of courtesy and concentration	**1**	**2**	**3**	**4**	**5**

TOTAL YOUR SCORE =

KEY TO INTERPRETATION:

There are three levels of listening — superficial, evaluative, and active.
Superficial listeners hear little and largely ignore what potential buyers are trying to say.
Evaluative listeners are listening to some extent, but put their own biases on what is being communicated to them.
Active listeners are truly engaged in the process of being influenced and will pay attention to both the message and the meaning behind the client's words.

If you scored 18–36 you are an Active listener.
If you scored 37–72 you are an Evaluative listener.
If you scored 73–90 you are an Superficial listener.

What Have You Learned?

His thoughts were slow
His words were few
And never made to glisten
But he was a joy
Wherever he went
You should have heard him listen.

UNKNOWN

After meeting a prospective customer, are you able to target his needs exactly? Do you know what hot buttons will trigger an enthusiastic "yes"? Consider these questions as a short list of information you should have about a prospective customer:

1. What industry is the client in?

_____

2. How is the industry performing?

_____

3. How long has the client's company been in business?

_____

4. What is their reputation in the marketplace?

5. What are their strengths?

6. What are their weaknesses?

7. How would you describe their management style?

8. How are buyers compensated?

9. What tend to be their most important criteria for buying?

10. How much loyalty do they have towards their vendors?

11. What role do they expect their vendors to play after the sale?

12. How receptive are they to ongoing product training and education?

13. Are their relationships with vendors short- or long-term?

14. Do they entertain long-term relationships?

15. How sophisticated are their information systems?

16. Who has supplied them with your product/service up to now?

17. What is their relationship like with alternative vendors?

18. Where do other vendors fall short?

_____

19. Who are the key decision-makers?

_____

20. What might motivate the key decision-makers to change vendors?

_____

21. What process does the organization go through in order to "register" a new vendor?

If you are an effective listener, you will have answered at least 75 percent of these questions in the affirmative. If you didn't you need to pay more attention!

4

Dealing with Objections

Preventing Objections

The sweetest words of pen or song
Are "You are right and I am wrong."

UNKNOWN

$\mathcal{E}$very salesperson is used to hearing "no." But the greatest salespeople don't believe that "no" means "no." Instead, they hear the potential client say, "I have yet to be convinced, and will change my mind when this happens."

It is easier to avoid objections than to deal with them. But sometimes objections should be welcomed since they give you insight into the thinking of your client. These insights will help you deal with issues, satisfy the client, and get the order.

Too many objections can create an acrimonious atmosphere that might prevent a win-win outcome. To ensure that the objections you do get are limited and useful for you to meet the needs of your client, avoid words that will create negative sentiments. The most risky are identified below.

1. "Buy" and "sell." People are always buying or selling and seldom enjoy the process. So switch to the term "own." People like to own something; it makes them feel secure.

2. *"Sign."* People don't like to *sign* contracts because it gives
    the feeling of being painted into a corner. It assumes finality,
    permanence, and inflexibility. Use the word "OK" or "confirm."
    For example, "Please OK our understanding" or "Would you
    confirm our Statement of Work?"

3. *"Contract."* This word conjures up images, like "signing" a
    one-sided deal, something that lawyers will need to look at,
    perhaps containing fine print that will prove to be ominous.
    A contract is very different from a handshake that suggests trust.
    Instead of asking someone to sign a contract, ask her to "OK
    our agreement" or "get the paperwork done."

4. *"Price," "payment," "cash," or "deposit."* These words connote
    giving rather than receiving. Use the word "invest" instead. For
    example, "By investing in this program, you will get better
    trained and motivated staff."

Overcoming Objections

If you don't argue with me, it means you haven't been listening.

UNKNOWN

An objection is a reason for not buying, arising from a prospect's lack of understanding. It is usually based on insufficient information. Objections are the food of good salespeople. They give you valuable insight into the psyche of the potential buyer. They lay out the extent of the obstacles you are facing and enable you to develop a game plan to solve such problems. Silence and a lack of communication are the salesperson's worst enemy. They give you nothing to work with and little chance of success. It is most unlikely that you will be able to sell to someone who doesn't have an objection.

1. The smart salesperson welcomes objections. It indicates interest. And, if you overcome those objections, your probability of a sale is much greater.

2. It is unlikely that you will find customers that have no objections. It's human nature to throw some obstacle in your path with the objective of gaining some advantage in return. On some occasions, however, you might find an unusually large number of roadblocks. This being the case, it is possible that you have made your standard "pitch" with little regard to the specific needs of the customer, made assumptions about the buyer's needs without confirming them, failed to establish any rapport, not asked for permission to make your pitch, or not done your homework. Research the company through the Web and other sources. Not doing so would indicate a lack of thoroughness and of interest in meeting the specific needs of the client.

When in this situation, rethink your approach and develop a new strategy. The easiest and best way is to ask questions such as "Does what I'm showing you meet your expectations?" or "Am I understanding this information differently from you?" These will give you a chance to find out what's going on in the buyer's mind and to consider what you're doing wrong.

3. If you regularly get objections from clients, you need to rethink your whole strategy. Are you being proactive and heading off as many objections as possible? Have you been listening? Consider these strategies:

- Deal with common objections in your presentation, but put a positive spin on them. For example, say, "While we realize that our price is higher than those of some of our competitors, we have also gone out of our way to justify the price differential by including these additional benefits . . ."
- Cover objections that are unspoken, but obvious from the body language of your potential buyer. By covering an issue that appears to bring some discomfort to the buyer, you are demonstrating your empathy and willingness to deal with issues in a constructive manner. This can be introduced: "You may have been wondering about . . . so let me tell you about it."

4. When an objection is raised, adopt the following strategy:

- Never argue. It's like getting into a boxing ring; you're going to get hit for sure. Treat each objection as a condition. Then find out if the condition is legitimate. For example, if the buyer says "I'm too old," ask "Why?" or "What makes you think so?" If they say "I don't have the money," ask "How much do you have?" or "How much do you think it would take?" If they say "There is no money in the budget," say "When are you going to be doing new budgets?"
- Recognize the question by thanking the person for raising the issue. You may say "I understand how you feel" or "I appreciate your concern."
- Clarify to make sure you fully understand. Say, "Let me make sure I understand that issue so that I can help you. Is it . . . ?" or "If I am clear about the issue, your concern is . . . Is that right?"
- Deal with their concern. Use one of the power strategies outlined below to deal with it.
  - Provide factual evidence to support your case (rationality).
  - Provide documented case studies and reference to support your position (legitimacy).
  - Show how other clients with similar issues have benefited from your product/service (precedent). Show reference letters.
  - Identify others in their industry that are getting ahead by using your product/service (competition).
  - Offer to rebate the full cost — if that is their concern — if they are not fully satisfied (risk-taking). Depending on the client, such an offer could be construed as confidence or desperation. This may cause you additional headaches as you may need to put your offer in writing.

- Confirm that the potential buyer has understood your point of view. "Have I made my point?"
- Confirm that they agree with you. "Do you agree?"

5. Never lie if you have no response to an objection. Always recognize that it is a tough and legitimate issue and then ask for time to research the issue and get back to the objector. Suggest a realistic time when this will be done.

6. Consider avoiding dealing with the objection. Some objections are simply an attempt to be argumentative. Responding might legitimize the issue. So acknowledge the objection by saying, "Yes, I understand how you feel about it, and let me . . ." You then proceed to deal with another issue. The issue may be forgotten because it wasn't valid. But if the objection is raised a second time, it probably is valid and needs to be dealt with. Alternatively, offer to come back to the issue.

7. Deal with the objection upfront and brag about it! You probably could anticipate the most commonly expressed objection in advance. So get it out of the way by turning it into a feature. For example, if the vehicle you are selling is small, you might say: "The vehicle would have been unacceptable a few years ago, but now North American consumers have wised up to the advantage of a car that uses space in ways we couldn't have even dreamed of, yet still offers the comfort of a much larger vehicle. It also looks great and is more economical than ever before."

Issues and Answers

There are two sides to every argument – until you take one.

LAWRENCE J. PETER

*H*ere are the most common objections and strategies to deal with them.

1. "The price is too high."

This is a frequent objection. Help solve the problem by asking open-ended questions such as "How did you arrive at this conclusion?" or "High compared to what?"

Based on the answer, work with the customer to prove that the price is in fact reasonable. Or find a way to ease the perceived financial burden such as leasing.

- Reduce the objection to make it seem ridiculous. For example, if the person is buying a computer and objects to the price, ask how overpriced he thinks it is. If he says $150, ask how long he intends to use it. The answer might be three years. Ask him to estimate the cost per year. Answer: $50 per year. Ask him to calculate the additional cost per day. Answer: about 13¢.

  Ask how many hours a day will he use it. Answer: 6 hours.

Ask what extra cost per hour would this amount to? Answer: about 2¢. Then point out, "Would you lose the opportunity to invest in a computer of this quality for 2¢ an hour?" Guess what will happen?

2. **"I always buy from your competitor and have been completely satisfied."**
Acknowledge her loyalty and share your understanding. Then through questioning, find out why she uses your competitor and why she chose them originally. Depending on her answers, find a way in which you can do better.
- "We are closer to you."
- "We deliver in less time."
- "We have made the most innovations to our product as you can see from this survey."

Ask the person to rate their supplier on a scale of 1 to 10. If she suggests anything less than 10, find out what it is that she is not getting and show how you can meet that particular need.

3. **"You're too far away from me."**
Change the way she sees distance. Move from kilometres to time. Even if your office is twice the distance, show that it takes the same amount of time to get to you.

4. **"I don't like _____ who works for you. He was rude to me."**
Show your concern and appreciation of his sentiments. Then suggest ways you can remedy the situation, bearing in mind that you have no control over another's personality. Alternatively, you might ask your customer. "If one of your employees behaved that way, what would you do?" Listen to his response and see if you can apply his solution.

5. "I don't like your product because it failed me in this way . . ."

Don't argue. Again, show empathy for her comments. Then ask, "Have you ever had a product of yours that failed to meet the needs of your customers? If so, what did you do about it?" Whatever she answers, respond by saying, "That's exactly what we are working on," assuming this to be true. If not, let her know that you'll bring her recommendation to your manager.

6. "I need to check with someone else."

Do two things. First, ask for the person's phone number. That way you can

- test whether the need to get approval is legitimate
- offer to assist in getting approval

Then find out

- whether the customer has approved the purchase and just needs the OK (In that case, offer to make the call.)
- whether the "someone else" is the *real* decision-maker (In that case, offer to phone and get the approval from her.)
- what criteria the *real* decision-maker has for giving the OK

Pricing Issues

What we obtain too cheap, we esteem too lightly.

THOMAS PAINE (1737–1809), ANGLO-AMERICAN POLITICAL THEORIST AND WRITER

One of the key needs of a customer is value. Value does not mean cheapness; it means creating the perception that there are sufficient benefits to justify the price you are charging.

Prices may go up or down. This can cause your client to be puzzled, surprised, annoyed, or even angry.

Here are the reasons for and strategies to deal with price changes.

1. The primary reasons for price changes include the following:
- *Technological changes.* Newer technological innovations are often more expensive since demand is initially high.
- *Obsolescence.* Prices may be cut on end-of-the-line products.
- *Quality improvement.* As mistakes, reworks, and returns are reduced, the increased efficiency can be passed on to the customer through lower prices.
- *Financial problems.* If an organization has a liquidity crunch, it may resort to price-cutting to reduce inventories quickly, turning them into cash.

- *Rationalization.* Improved work processes can lead to dramatic cost reductions, some or all of which can be passed on to the customer.
- *Competitive pressures.* The market might simply not allow change to a premium without being able to demonstrate some added-value advantage.

2. In the event of a significant price change — up or down — be sure to do the following:
   - Explain why. Be rational in showing why there has been an increase. Provide factual data instead of opinion-based discussion. If your price has *declined*, show the client the advantage, trying to link the change to project a customer focus.
   - Help the client overcome problems associated with the price increase. Suggest, for example, that they
     - order before the increase
     - order more to take advantage of a bulk discount
     - do a promotion to ensure that inventory clearance helps their bottom line
     - consider other ways of saving money such as alternative delivery methods, less expensive packaging, using their staff for some of the process, etc.

Here are some strategies to deal with "sticker shock":

1. Stay away from price resistance levels. Charging $99.99 seems so much easier to deal with than $100. The difference is inconsequential, but psychologically significant.

2. Amortize the price. Instead of quoting $10,000, consider selling on the basis of $500 per month. If you need an example, just think of the popularity of lease finance on premium vehicles.

3. Quote a price range to give the client time to adjust. Suggest a price range that is not too broad, such as $12,000 to $14,000. If you quote $10,000 to $15,000 it might suggest to the client that you are testing them for acceptance and are likely to "load" the price if they do not protest.

4. Avoid roundup prices. If you are doing a significant job for a client, and quote $10,000 or $100,000, they are likely to feel that you've rounded up the price and built a lot of "fat" into it. A price of $9,400 or $98,700 sounds far more legitimate.

Convincing Strategies

Sales Aids

A first-rate soup is better than a second-rate painting.

ABRAHAM MASLOW (1908–70), AMERICAN PSYCHOLOGIST

Anything that can enhance the effectiveness of a sales presentation should be used. Here are some tips on how to make effective use of sales aids.

1. Sales aids are designed to improve the effectiveness of your message. They do the following:
- show that you are prepared
- carry a message of interest to the potential buyer
- reinforce your spoken message with a visual message
- increase the legitimacy of your message
- demonstrate that you are professional
- paint a picture that would otherwise be difficult to communicate

2. Sales aids are the additional props that enhance a presentation of your ideas. The most widely used sales aids include
- laptop presentations

- PowerPoint presentations using an LCD projection system
- paper-based presentations from a flip-file

3. To be most effective, sales aids should
   - be consistently up-to-date
   - look new, never worn
   - speak for themselves

4. Sales aids are most useful if they
   - provoke discussion
   - give the client time to internalize the message without being interrupted
   - support the presentation rather than dominating it

5. Keep your presentation simple. Make sure that each point is short and easily understood.

6. Give your sales aids a personal touch by customizing them with the logo of the client.

Demonstrations

Seeing is believing.

*N*ot every product or service lends itself to be demonstrated. But those that do — such as software, tools and gadgets — sell significantly better if demonstrated.

1. A good demonstration will
- reinforce the message of the salesperson
- take only as long as is needed
- allow time for questions
- be paced at the speed that the potential buyer can absorb
- involve the potential buyer
- be systematic, with an appropriate introduction and conclusion
- be easily understood

2. Key points to remember before you demonstrate are these:
- Be prepared. Have a checklist to ensure that you take all necessary props with you.
- Set up quickly. Get to your appointment early so that you

can set up beforehand if possible. If not, have a way of setting up as inconspicuously as possible. Make it look easy.

- Be clear. Avoid language that might impress, but will not be understood. Avoid jargon. Always confirm understanding if you are not sure about the effectiveness of the message.
- Have a backup plan if your equipment doesn't work. If it can go wrong, it probably will. Don't sweat, look embarrassed, or apologize. Make the presentation appear as "normal" as possible. Don't point out what you cannot do. Simply continue with what you can.
- Make it look easy.
- Make it fun.

Preparing for
Presentations

Blessed are those who can laugh at themselves,
for they shall never cease to be amused.

UNKNOWN

$\mathcal{W}$hen you have to give a presentation, everything depends on your ability to get your point across coherently and convincingly. Whether or not you succeed will depend largely on how well you prepare.

Here's how to get ready:

1. Consider your strengths.
- What makes you attractive as a presenter? Are you knowledgeable? articulate? Use these strengths to your advantage.
- What sort of bond do you already have with the audience? Do you have background or experiences in common? Play on these things to highlight your connection to your listeners. You can also refer to those members of the audience with some sort of authority.

2. Ask yourself what you want to convince people to do. Then calculate how specific you will have to be to get them to do it. If you give them too little information they may be unable to do what you want; if you give them too much you may bore or insult them.

3. Most presentations end up longer than planned, so keep it short. Remember:
   - People get bored quickly — the average attention span is only minutes.
   - If you try to communicate too much, people will get confused and remember nothing.

4. Ask yourself what your audience wants. Are they after inspiration? entertainment? Do they want only facts, or are they looking for leadership and new ideas? Your objective should match their expectations. Organize your presentation to satisfy them.

5. Whatever your main idea is, have an apt metaphor or analogy to illustrate it.

6. Don't start preparing the night before the presentation. The more time you give yourself, the more material you'll be able to incorporate and the better your thinking will be.
   - When you're brainstorming, put all your new ideas in one place.
   - Draft them onto Post-it notes and stick them to the wall so that you can see them all at once.
   - Cluster the notes into coherent groups.
   - Decide on the order the idea-groups will be presented.

- Write the primary ideas on index cards in large, easy-to-read letters. You are not going to read your presentation. But these cards will remind you where you are in your speech and where you're going.

7. Practise your presentation out loud. Stand up when you rehearse, and practise your body language — stand erect, with your chest out. This posture will make you feel and look more confident.

8. Write out a list of things you will need on the big day.

9. Scout the room in which you'll be delivering your presentation. Is there anything that could pose a problem? Are the acoustics all right? Is there somewhere to plug in your projector or laptop?

10. Finally, visualize success. Picture an audience enthralled and impressed. If you have prepared adequately, that's what they'll be.

Reducing Stage Fright

Fear is a question. What are you afraid of and why? Our fears are a treasure house of self-knowledge if we explore them.

MARILYN FRENCH, AMERICAN AUTHOR AND CRITIC

It's normal to be nervous when addressing a large audience. But there is no reason to be terrified — as most North Americans are. Studies have shown that people are more afraid of making a speech than they are of death! But if you avoid making presentations, which you will be called upon to do more and more as your career takes off, you will be squandering opportunities. When the spotlight is on you, it's your turn to shine. Seize the moment. And while it is unlikely you'll ever be totally relaxed, you can easily reduce your anxiety. Here's how:

1. Use the adrenaline rush to make yourself sharp. It can improve your performance.

2. Confidence will take the edge off your fear. The following are some techniques to stoke your confidence:
   - Prepare rigorously. The more you rehearse your presentation, the more confident you'll be.

- Psych yourself up. Visualize success. If you fear a bored, indifferent audience, picture your listeners blown away by your knowledge and enthusiasm.
- Give yourself a pep talk. Make personal affirmations starting with "I." I am confident. I am an expert. I am the person to get this job done.
- Give yourself stepping stones. Pencil in your flipchart notes so that you can read them while the audience cannot. Highlight your overheads so that you won't forget where you're going in the heat of the moment. If you're speaking from a lectern, write out notes on index cards.
- Find a few friendly faces in the audience and focus on them. You'll be able to turn to them for support.

3. Speak only on topics you have some enthusiasm for. If you aren't charged up, your audience won't be excited either.

4. Begin your presentation with something you and the audience are familiar with. You'll all feel more comfortable and fall into a comfortable rapport.

5. Memorize the first few moments of your presentation. If you start off right, you'll be fine.

6. Never read. Reading sounds monotonous. Your audience will wonder why you didn't just hand out photocopies of your presentation. Stick to your index cards. You will need between eight and twelve for a half-hour talk.

Features, Advantages, and Benefits

Have you ever found yourself making a great presentation without a sale? It happens all the time! Problem is, few people buy because you're offering interesting or even wonderful features. A few may buy because there are some advantages to your offering. But most buying is done because of benefits. This being so, let us examine each in the context of the sales process.

1. A feature is any physical characteristic of a product. Features can include

- colour
- size
- shape
- content
- packaging
- technical specification
- delivery

2. Features contain little persuasive ability. They simply describe what you are offering. To get the potential buyer interested, you need to let the person know what the advantages of those features are. Describing advantages typically follows a rundown of the features. Possible advantages might be that the product runs faster, is more powerful, is more appealing, or has greater flexibility.

3. Customers buy on perceived value: "What return will I get on my investment?" Many customers see all vendors as having similar offerings. To distinguish your solution, you need to be able to link benefits to those key needs of the customer. The more you are able to show that your solution has added value, the higher the probability of a sale.

- A benefit can be in one of many forms: increased profits, higher sales, improved market share, increased competitiveness, reduced costs, improved productivity, increased convenience, enhanced customer loyalty, improved security, increased peace of mind, and increased customer satisfaction.
- A benefit is only a benefit if the customer sees it as one. Without benefits, a feature has little or no value. For example, having a computer with a 128K modem allows someone to download information off the Internet faster than lower-K modems. Lead-free paint offers health-related benefits, in-line skates offer the benefits of getting fresh outdoor air and exercise, and a V8 engine offers the benefit of being able to pull a boat with ease.
- Identifying benefits for potential buyers means relating the product/service to their needs and increasing sales.
- Typical psychological needs that you should consider relating to include
  - vanity
  - security
  - desire to succeed
  - loss prevention

Negotiating:

Win-Win Tactics

The nice thing about egos is that everyone has one.

JOE GIRARD, *HOW TO CLOSE EVERY SALE*

Organizations are created for the long term. Salespeople promote longevity by creating and sustaining long-term relationships with all stakeholders based on mutual gains and trust.

New relationships, such as strategic partnerships or sole supplier, often begin with negotiation. The end result needs to be good for both parties. Anything but a win-win outcome will come back to haunt you. Here's how to produce a mutually beneficial result:

1. Situations in which salespeople find they must negotiate include
- creating an agreement for outsourcing of a product or service
- adjusting to new prices or other terms
- changing terms of delivery
- determining salary and other compensation details
- purchasing of a vehicle
- changing deadlines for reports

2. Before you begin formal negotiations, do this:

- Prepare yourself thoroughly. This will reduce your stress level and give you the ability to display confidence.
- Develop a list of alternative outcomes. Evaluate them all. Select the best plus some acceptable fallback positions that could still meet your needs.

3. At the start of your negotiations, do this:

- Establish a goal that is good for both parties. Even if the parameters are broad, both parties should focus on a similar objective instead of beating each other up.
- Establish ground-rules for the process. Doing so is particularly useful if the negotiation might be emotional. Agreements could include
  - listening to each other without interruption
  - respecting each other even though you may disagree on issues
  - being flexible on the less important issues
  - tackling one issue at a time
  - agreeing on the trivial issues first and leaving the more difficult ones to last
- State your needs clearly and firmly. Make sure that the other party understands them by getting verbal confirmation.
- Determine what the other party's needs are. If you can meet their needs, chances are they will be more inclined to meet yours. If you frustrate them, they will do the same to you. Find out what their needs are by listening and asking open-ended questions. Listen to what they are telling you instead of formulating rebuttals. If you are not sure, ask them to repeat or paraphrase their words to confirm understanding.

4. During negotiations, do this:

- Build on the things you agree on. Look for other, similar areas that you can agree on.
- Prioritize issues; determine what is negotiable and what is not.
- Try to understand what the other negotiators think and feel. Read their non-verbal language. What are their facial expressions telling you? What are their eyes doing when you ask for commitment? And what are their postures and hand gestures telling you?
- Avoid arguing, especially on minor issues. Train yourself to agree to the small things so that you establish a collaborative environment focused on solving the more important items.
- Avoid aggressive behaviour. This will result in a win-lose outcome. This behaviour is typified by
  - talking louder than the other person
  - dominating the discussion
  - using sarcasm
  - using authority (if you have it) to force the other party into acquiescence
- Avoid passive behaviour. This behaviour is characterized by
  - refusing to deal with the issues
  - failing to make others aware of your concerns
- Be assertive. Be tough (not unreasonable) on the issues, but soft on people. Being assertive means that you will
  - maintain eye contact
  - speak with a firm voice
  - use "I" statements, not "you" statements
- Avoid blaming others. You don't want to poison the atmosphere and cloud the focus on problem solving.

- Don't say "no" without giving your reasons for declining a proposal.
- Don't dwell on the past. The past can't be undone. Being stuck in the past will cause hostility and defensiveness.
- Look to the future. Visualize how much better things will be if both parties are able to get satisfaction.
- Probe. Ask questions. Listen. In this way, you will uncover the needs of the other person. By finding those needs and then meeting them, you will set the stage for meeting your needs.
- Show positive body language. Don't fold your arms or legs, roll your eyes, tense your body, scowl, or raise your voice.
- Seek creative solutions that satisfy both parties.
  - Avoid "either/or" solutions. Limiting yourself to two alternatives reduces the possibility of creative new solutions.
  - Use the words "what if?"
  - Focus on common interests rather than opinions.
- The party with the shortest deadlines will tend to concede more as the deadline approaches. So if you have a deadline, don't reveal it.
- Deal with issues as they arise so that they don't accumulate and overwhelm your discussion.
- Don't get side-tracked. If your negotiations are going off on a tangent, get back on track with a comment such as "Yes, I can relate to that, but could we get back to the central issue . . . "
- Be creative. There is more than one way to reach your goal. Have alternative ideas that will still provide benefits for all. Rigidity reduces creative problem solving and increases conflict.
- Stop negotiations from time to time to share your feelings. Find out how others are feeling. If anyone's feelings are negative, find ways to overcome the hostility so that you can continue to solve problems in a constructive manner.

- Whenever the discussion becomes vague, clarify your understanding with a summary. For example, say, "Do I understand the problem correctly? In my mind, it is . . . "
- In a unionized environment, be aware of items affected by the collective agreement. These should not be negotiated on a one-to-one basis.

5. At the conclusion of the negotiation, do this:
- Don't make extra concessions during the euphoria of reaching an agreement.
- Summarize everyone's understanding so that everyone is absolutely clear as to what has been agreed upon. Reduce it to writing so that no one will have to rely on memory for the details.

No power is strong enough to be long lasting if it labours under the weight of fear.

MARCUS TULLIUS CICERO (106–43 BC), ROMAN ORATOR

Negotiating:

Using Your Power to Influence the Buyer

The measure of a man is what he does with power.

PITTACUS (C. 650–C. 570 BC), GREEK STATESMAN AND MILITARY LEADER

Salespeople are in the business of influence. They are influencing people daily. For example, they need to persuade

- buyers to use their product/service
- support staff to assist with clerical duties
- people in other areas to ensure that promises made are delivered

Negotiating is the ability to influence people. It is the art of letting someone else have your way. Most people have no idea how easy it is to influence others.

People have a lot more power to influence than they believe. There are many ways you can use power to help you achieve your objective. The more power you have, the more likely you are to be persuasive. So find your power in some of the following sources:

1. **Precedent.** Show examples of where your product/service has added value for other clients.

2. **Legitimacy.** Legitimacy is about appearance. The most legitimate ideas are those that are
- presented in writing
- endorsed by experts
- appear in official places and prestigious magazines

So, present your ideas with supporting documentation such as references. Point to articles in publications that speak to the virtues of your product/service. Quote well-known people who have endorsed similar ideas to yours.

3. **Persistence.** If water keeps dropping onto a rock, it will eventually make a hole in it. Similarly, you will wear down your opposition if you are tenacious. You will demonstrate persistence by not taking "no" for an answer. Keep wearing your opponent down with comments like "Yes, but . . ." or "When else could we meet?" or "Let's keep trying till we do find a way."

4. **Competition.** Let potential clients know that *they* are competing for your services, not the other way around. For example, they should feel that you have limited inventory and resources that are in demand by others.

5. **Knowledge.** Let people know about your expertise. Show them your qualifications (legitimacy). The more impressed they are with your credentials, the easier it will be to influence them. Also, demonstrate your knowledge with facts and examples of where you have been successful before (precedent).

6. **Rationality.** Give people the data to back up your opinions. Presenting the data in writing (legitimacy) will further increase your power.

7. **Rank.** The more senior you are in your organization, the more power you will have. For example, a senior salesperson will be more influential than a junior one. The director of sales will have more power than a salesperson and the vice-president will have more power than anyone other than the president. So, depending on the size and strategic nature of the transaction, consider bringing in the "big guns."

6

People Issues

Selling to Different Personalities

If you don't sell, it's not the product that's wrong, it's you.

ESTÉE LAUDER, COSMETICS EXECUTIVE

The human species is very complex. Each of us thinks differently. We have our own way of making decisions and have a unique need to be able to influence people and events. By understanding your potential buyer better and adjusting your style to suit him, you increase your chances of influencing him. If you find your style and the buyer's style similar, your chances of success increase dramatically. If your styles are different and you make no adjustment, your probability of a sale declines measurably.

A useful (though oversimplified) model of personality classification comes from Carl Jung, who believed that every person is predominantly one of these four types:

- feeling
- thinking
- intuitive
- sensing

1. **Feeling people.** They make decisions based on people. You will notice that they

- enjoy chit-chat
- are as interested in you as they are in what service or product you offer
- need to see a human value to their purchase
- need to feel comfortable with you before reviewing what you have to offer

You can spot a feeler by noticing

- items of a personal nature in their office, such as family photos and mementoes
- decorations that show people more than things
- an emphasis on people in their communications
- a preference to meet in a more informal setting, away from the office
- a focus on benefits for people
- a tendency to be more open to listening and compromise

To influence feeling people you should

- show the benefits of your product/service to the human side of the organization
- avoid a strong emphasis on monetary benefits
- behave in an open, warm, and friendly way
- take an interest in the buyer on a personal level

2. **Thinking people.** They make decisions based on logic. They prefer

- appearing impersonal
- focusing on the bottom line
- being brief and businesslike
- analyzing the smallest details

You can spot a thinker, as thinkers tend to
- be neatly and conservatively dressed
- have more electronic gadgets than others
- ask tough questions
- appear blunt and "to the point"

To influence thinkers, you need to
- get to the point quickly
- prove your case with figures, charts, and facts
- prove your case based on merit
- dress conservatively

3. **Intuitive people.** They are forward-looking and tend to be creative in their problem solving. They are distinguished by
- creativity
- keen intellect
- interest in "the big picture"

You can spot an intuitive person by noticing
- her questions, which focus on issues rather than details
- the reference or philosophy books on her shelves
- the abstract art and charts on the wall

To influence intuitive people, you need to
- describe benefits in relation to the long-term future
- describe benefits in general terms
- show her how your product/service fits into the overall strategy of the client organization
- allow time for her to imagine benefits

4. **Sensing people.** They tend to operate in the world by making effective use of their five senses: taste, touch, smell, sight, and hearing. They tend to be
- detail-oriented

- decisive
- pragmatic
- impatient

You can spot a sensing person because he

- focuses on what's in front of him instead of on the future
- thinks aloud (talks before thinking)
- usually has a messy office
- is surrounded by action pictures on the wall
- dresses more casually, without a jacket or tie

To influence sensing people, you need to

- focus on getting things done, suggesting action steps
- be brief and to the point
- show examples, allowing him to see, touch, and smell (if appropriate) what you are offering
- present only viable options to expedite decision-making

Communication:

Avoiding Breakdowns

*Effective communication is 20% what you know
and 80% how you feel about what you know.*

JIM ROHN

*G*etting on the same wavelength as the buyer is key to closing a sale. Here are the most common causes of a communication breakdown:

1. **Problem:** Distractions

Sometimes the sale is taking place in a busy area, such as an open workspace or restaurant, with lots of things happening around. People might be stopping to converse with your buyer. All of this will prevent her from giving you her full attention.
Solution: Maintain eye contact, raise your voice slightly, and ask the buyer a question to confirm her understanding.

2. **Problem:** A disorganized presentation

Your presentation will cause the buyer to become agitated if you
- do not follow a step-by-step sequence
- can't find the appropriate documents
- are presenting generic, rather than customized, information

Solution: Stop! Ask the buyer if you can use the washroom. Take the time to think about what you are doing wrong, clear your head, and go back. Then describe to the buyer what you would like to do (don't apologize, as this will draw attention to your incompetence!). Then, start again and keep asking for confirmation anytime the buyer's body language suggests that he is losing interest again.

3. **Problem:** Information overload
Your buyer may not be a detail person, nor may he need the level of detail you are presenting. Don't bore him!
Solution: Explain the level of detail you can go into and confirm that this would be of interest.

4. **Problem:** Poor listening
If you fail to understand the needs of the client, you may as well be talking to a wall.
Solution: Stop talking. Listen. Ask open-ended questions and keenly observe non-verbal cues.

5. **Problem:** Undue sales pressure
You may be under pressure to produce sales. The buyer is not. If your badgering does not stop, you will lose the sale.
Solution: Slow down. Back off. Give the buyer some space and time to think. Then ask questions to find where she is at and work with her to deal with outstanding issues.

6. **Problem:** No need for your product/service
Carrying coal to Newcastle is pointless.
Solution: Move on to people who may have a need. Thank the person for his time and ask whether he knows of anyone who could use your product/service.

7. **Problem:** Perceptual barriers

You may be operating on a totally different wavelength if you and the buyer see things from different cultural perspectives. **Solution:** If you don't understand your buyer, listen more. Ask questions until you have a clear picture of their frame of reference. And next time, research that type of buyer, especially if they are becoming increasingly important to you. Alternatively, pass them on to a colleague who does understand them.

8. **Problem:** Overly sophisticated concepts

A presentation that is too technical may go over the head of the buyer, causing frustration and feelings of inadequacy. **Solution:** Use the KISS principle — Keep It Short and Simple. But don't treat people like children. Know your client's level of understanding and make your pitch accordingly.

9. **Problem:** Complicated language

When talking to clients, avoid trying to impress them with words and language that they can't understand. If you do, they'll wonder about the meaning and be too embarrassed to ask. In turn, your idea might be lost. **Solution:** Use everyday language. Make sure that the buyer understands you by asking specific questions from time to time.

Difficult People:

How to Handle Them

To handle yourself, use your head.
To handle others, use your heart.

ELEANOR ROOSEVELT (1884–1962), AMERICAN HUMANITARIAN

$\mathcal{S}$ alespeople can come into conflict with people at every turn, from secretaries who "protect" their bosses, to distribution people who might have different priorities about delivery, to accounts payable people who are delaying payment on bills. Learning how to work with people that are intransigent is important. So, here are some ideas to deal with people who may be standing in your way:

1. The easiest way to handle difficult people is to avoid them
if you can. Watch out for those who
   - rejoice when you stumble
   - make decisions without consulting you
   - cut you off when you're speaking, particularly at meetings
   - bad-mouth others when they're not around; such people
     probably do the same behind your back
   - exaggerate, mislead, obfuscate, and otherwise lie
   - put their own priorities ahead of the group's

2. Since you can't always avoid these people, here's how to deal with them:

- Find out their good qualities — there must be some! — and stay focused on those.
- If the positive qualities are hard to identify, avoid dealing with such people in person or on the phone. Use your fax or e-mail to do the dirty work, or send a note.

3. If avoidance is impossible and you have to deal with the personality conflict head-on, try these techniques:

- Focus on the issues. Avoid personal criticism, as this will probably only provoke more of the behaviour you dislike.
- Give some feedback. Let the other person know what's going on. This is very sensitive stuff, so tread carefully. But well-considered feedback should make things better rather than worse.
- Before you criticize someone else, ask yourself whether you are blameless. Perhaps others find you as problematic as you find them. Make an effort to improve yourself and those around you will reciprocate.
- You must have *something* in common with the people you don't like. Find it. You may not be so different after all. And the better you know the person, the better you'll be able to understand him.

4. At least do no harm. Treating others with respect is at least a form of damage control. At best you have done unto others as you would have done unto you. There's much to be said for that.

Angry Customers

Anger is only one letter short of danger.

ELEANOR ROOSEVELT (1884–1962), AMERICAN HUMANITARIAN

One hopes never to let down a customer. But from time to time, promises will be broken for reasons you may not have had control over. This could compromise your customer and make her very angry. Here is a step-by-step process to deal with these situations:

1. Listen. Don't be defensive. And never, never argue. Allow the customer to explain the reason for her anger and give her time to vent. Don't interrupt. Listen to get as much information as possible, enabling you to clearly define the problem. Listening also allows the customer to ventilate, which will make her feel better, as she has got the issue off her chest and has been listened to.

2. Empathize. Show that you care. Better still, show that you understand. Never use the word "but." It indicates denial and an inability to understand the issue from the customer's perspective.

3. Find out more specifics so that you can get to the bottom of the issue. Ask these questions:

- "What happened?"
- "What were your expectations?"
- "How would you like us to fix it?"

4. Confirm. Summarize your understanding of the customer's issue. You can say, "So let me be sure I really understand. What I've heard you say is _____. Is that right?"

5. Resolve the issue. Tell the customer specifically what you will do to help them and when it will be done.

6. Confirm. Make sure that the customer is satisfied with your solution.

7. Follow up. After you have addressed the issue, follow up with the customer to ensure that her expectations have been met. Assure her of your ongoing desire to meet her expectations.

7

Closing

Closing the Sale

The most important thing in sales is to ask for the order.

JACK CAHAN

Salespeople don't get paid for building relationships with prospective customers. They get paid for securing orders. The average salesperson closes a sale on their fifth attempt! So it is critical that you have a variety of strategies to

- improve your chances of closing
- close in fewer attempts

Your prospecting is of no value unless you can close the sale. Here are some strategies to improve your chances dramatically:

1. Work with the customer carefully and skilfully throughout the sales process. Only then will you arrive at the final step — closing. Closing is a process that starts from the time you greet a prospect.

2. Start the closing process as soon as you can. However, timing
is everything. Your chances of closing the deal will be greatly
enhanced if you do it at the appropriate moment. Look for signals
that suggest he is ready to give you the OK. For example:
- a change in body language such as
  - leaning forward
  - smiling
  - nodding
- the asking of appropriate questions such as
  - "When do I have to pay?"
  - "When can I take delivery?"
  - "Can I get it in _____ colour?"

3. Watch carefully for buying signals. Attempting to close before the
prospect is ready may lead to anger and distrust. Buying signals
come in many forms, the most important of which are key words
("When could I get delivery?") or actions (the prospect trying out
a product that he had previously refused to touch).

4. Ask for the order. Find out where you stand by getting feedback
from the client. Say, "Why don't I write up the order?" or "Let's
summarize the terms of the order, OK?"

5. Assert yourself. If the prospective client is having difficulty
making a decision, help her by telling her what you intend to
do. For example, "I'm going to install the system by next
Friday, OK?"

6. Focus on benefits, not features. Ensure that the benefits have
been clearly articulated and are linked to those described by the

customer. The more measurable the benefits, the more compelling your case. For example, suggest, "If we proceed today, I'll ensure that I am able to meet your budgetary limitations."

7. Trade benefits. Show how both parties can gain from the contract. Say, "If we can deliver the extra dozen, we'll be able to reduce your costs by 15 percent. Shall we go ahead?"

8. Give options that all lead to a close. Say, "Which do you want, the red or the green?"

9. Make a concession. Give something to get something. Say, "If I can fast-track the delivery, will you be able to give me the OK now?"

10. Close with confidence, referring to key information the customer has provided you, summarizing benefits.

Closing Techniques

*Salespeople don't get paid for talking to prospects . . .
they get paid for selling (closing) them!*

ROBERT L. SHOOK, CO-AUTHOR, *THE COMPLETE PROFESSIONAL SALESMAN*

*T*here are many popular and effective closes. No one is better than the next. Each can work well depending on the situation you are in and your ability to execute them effectively. Learn and practise them all to make them part of your repertoire.

1. The divide-and-conquer close

If you have two people you are selling to, one is more likely to be positive than the other. So, focus on the most supportive person while making the assumption that the more negative person is in agreement.

2. The minor-major close

Tugboats work hard at getting large ships into harbour. And they do so by nudging and pulling a little at a time. The same process works in a sales situation. Do a little at a time. Getting agreement to many minor decisions will eventually lead to agreement on the major issue. Selling an insurance policy is easier if you get agreement to the sum of money available, the frequency of payments, the method of payment, and the beneficiary. "Yes" responses to these issues will automatically lead to a signature on the application without having to ask for a go-ahead.

3. The "assuming the sale is closed" close

This is one of the best closing techniques, and perhaps the most frequently used. Assume you have the order from the outset. Always use language that suggests that you are going to do business with the buyer and that your discussions are simply about sorting out the details. For example, say, "Let's figure out the schedule so that we can proceed."

4. The paddock close

Ever heard the expression "as stubborn as a mule"? Well, a horse is a first cousin to the mule and pretty obstinate, too. Imagine trying to get a horse to pose for a perfect picture with one leg forward. To get the perfect picture, the photographer might try walking him around the paddock and trying again, hoping that the horse will have forgotten its stubbornness. The same works for a client who seems to have an entrenched position. After trying to close, change topics and then try to close again. If you're rebuffed, do it all again — change the topic till you have an opportunity to try again.

5. The "that won't stop you" close

Don't take "no" as being "no." Take "no" as being "maybe." Just assume that the customer is still going to say "yes" by saying, *"That won't stop you, will it?"*

6. The Vince Lombardi close

The legendary coach Vince Lombardi instilled in his team a desire to win and never quit. In sales, being tenacious and refusing to quit can pay big dividends. So, make another effort.

7. The silent close

After you make a proposal, shut up! The first to speak loses. You will get a "yes" or an objection, each of which must be dealt with differently. If it's a "yes," proceed to get the details of delivery. If "no," treat the objection as useful information that will enable you to solve the problem and then close.

8. The conditional close

Customers will often throw roadblocks at you, either to give them time to think or avoid closing. A typical example is "We don't have money in the budget" or "I'll need to get my boss to approve." You can close the sale by saying, "Let me understand you correctly. You are telling me that everything is fine save for this one issue. So, you will go ahead if I can resolve this issue for you. Is that correct?" The secret to this close is to first get the customer's commitment to buy if you can satisfactorily respond to a single objection.

9. The Ben Franklin validation close

Benjamin Franklin had a system for decision making. He would create a list of pros and cons. If the pros exceeded the cons, he would decide for the idea; if not, he would reject it. He would use a piece of paper with a line down the middle and the items listed on either side. The Ben Franklin validation close is achieved by following this step-by-step process:

- Give the piece of paper and your pen to the client, and ask them to list all the advantages first. Help them. Create as long a list as possible, numbering them as you do.
- Next, ask the client to list the disadvantages and stay silent! They will invariably identify very few (four would be a lot).
- Ask the client, "What does this analysis now show?" Allow them to state the obvious — that they need to proceed with the sale.

10. The negative yes close

Ask what you have done wrong. They will define the issues better for you so that you can deal with them. Ask them a series of questions, all of which will elicit a "no" answer, which really means "yes" to the sale. For example, "Is it the reputation of my company that concerns you?" Answer: "No." Or, "Are the terms that we're providing you not fair?" Answer: "No." After enough negative answers, you can try to close with a more direct proposal: "Since you are satisfied with the company, product, and service, tell me where we can deliver it to."

11. The limited offer close

Letting the buyer know that she has limited time to take advantage of the situation may enable you to get commitment to conclude the sale. Typically, you might say, "This item is on special until 5 p.m. today, after which its price will be increased by 30 percent." Needless to say, you should not lie to make the sale and should have the ability to back up your statement.

12. The blank order close

Don't ask for permission to do so, but begin to take details starting with low-risk items such as address, phone numbers, etc., graduating to key issues such as delivery dates. When all the details are complete, don't ask the buyer to agree, but merely to confirm the details by signing the order.

13. The similar situation story close

Recall a story that will tug at the emotional strings of the buyer. It can be a good or heartbreaking story. Either way, you want the potential buyer to either be like the person in your story (a success) or avoid it (someone who didn't buy and became a disaster). For example, imagine yourself selling a vehicle at year-end. You might tell the story of someone who didn't take advantage of the sale price and had to settle for a lesser vehicle a month later when prices increased beyond his budget.

14. The repeat call close

If you are unable to close because the buyer expresses a desire to "sleep on it," then make a follow-up appointment right away. At the follow-up meeting, avoid asking for a "yes" or "no" response. Instead, do this:

- Begin by telling him something new, no matter what it is.
- Proceed to repeat your entire sales presentation, taking great pains to summarize all your previous agreements. Only allow the person to interrupt if signalling an intent to buy (which includes an objection).

15. The lost sales apology close

When everything is lost, pause at the door and apologize — sincerely — for having made such a poor presentation. After all, there can be no other reason for the potential client not to have given you the order other than your inability to present the issues properly. Now you are upset that this company cannot benefit from your service. Ask what it was that you did wrong so that you don't make the same mistake again. Based on the response you get, you may be able to identify a problem that you can overcome.

16. The secondary question closing

This close works as follows: you pose the major question, and before the client responds, follow up with a minor question. An example would be "When should we start the training, this month or next?" and then add, "Would you like the training to be done in-house or at a local hotel?" When the client makes a minor choice, the major issue of buying becomes automatic.

17. The sharp angle close

If a prospect asks about a desired feature, don't answer directly. Instead, respond, "Would you want it if it does have that feature?" If the answer is "yes," the sale is done, if indeed the product can perform the desired function or has the needed feature.

18. The "I'll think it over" close

Particularly with larger decisions, people will express their uncertainty about committing. This happens constantly. Confirm their interest by saying, "I just want to be clear that you need time to think because you are serious, right? You're not saying this just to get rid of me?" If they say "yes" — which they probably will — then get them to define specifically their objection by asking about specific issues such as "Is it the price/delivery/colour that you need to consider?" Keep trying until you find a specific issue that is unresolved. If there isn't an issue, try to close again. If there is an issue, ask if they would like you to solve it. If they say "yes," then try to solve their concern. You should then be able to close with the "blank order close."

Note: Many of the ideas in this chapter have been adapted from Roger Dawson's *Power Negotiating for Salespeople* tapes. These tapes are available from Nightingale-Conant Corporation, 1-800-323-5552.

Partnership Selling

Partnership Selling
Overview

Many people will walk in and out of your life.
But only true friends will leave footprints in your heart.

ELEANOR ROOSEVELT (1884–1962), AMERICAN HUMANITARIAN

*S*ales are the lifeblood of organizations. As such, this process is too important to be the sole responsibility of one person or department. It must be the collective responsibility of the entire company.

The function and approach of salespeople are evolving rapidly. Here are the major trends:

1. **Behind-the-counter selling.** This is typical of small towns where people are obliged to travel to a store to identify and pay for goods. The needs of customers are well defined.

2. **Away-from-the-counter selling.** In this scenario, the salesperson seeks out customers, peddling his product or service. The relationship is seldom harmonious and the salesperson typically relies on a variety of coercive strategies to close a sale.

$3.$ **Customer-driven sales.** Instead of "creating" a need, this approach requires that salespeople research the needs of the customer and fill those needs. It requires excellent listening, questioning, and empathy skills.

$4.$ **Partnership selling.** The most complex form of selling requires a long-term commitment and partnership between the buyer and seller. It is typified by

- desire to help the customer achieve their strategic business goals
- detailed understanding of the client's organization
- an integrated team approach to service all aspects of the relationship
- continuous evaluation, problem solving, and improvement
- measurement of the benefits and changes, to ensure ongoing evaluation, celebration, and problem solving
- trust

Choosing a Partner

Cooperation is spelt with two letters: WE.

UNKNOWN

*C*onverting from short-term, one-off sales to partnership selling is a strategic decision. Making the commitment to a new process requires significant changes to the organization in terms of the people that are employed, how they are organized and rewarded, the philosophy of the customer service, the need for secrecy, and the mentality of working collaboratively with others, to name just a few of the issues.

Before deciding whether to enter into a partnership arrangement with another organization, these issues need to be investigated:

1. **Finances.** How profitable is the potential partner? Take a look at the organization's annual report (if available) to see if you can spot problems that you could help address. What is the trend line of profits? Do their costs seem to be higher than those in the industry? Are their sales in decline?

2. **Competition.** How is the potential partner doing in the marketplace? Are their sales growing or declining? What is their market share? What have their major competitors done to improve their position in the marketplace? What innovative strategies have their competitors used to jump ahead?

3. **Market trends.** How is the industry doing? Is it expanding or in decline? Why is this so? What could you do to help the potential partner outperform the industry averages?

4. **Organization.** How is the potential partner's business organized? Is it hierarchical or flat? (It is easier to do business with an organization that is flat and flexible.) Is the organization structured along product or process lines? (Organizations structured around processes tend to be more customer focused and therefore more disposed to partnerships that benefit their customers.)

5. **Regulations.** Does the potential partner operate in a highly regulated industry? Are there government pressures that, if enforced, could reduce the partner's effectiveness? Are there things that you could do to reduce their dependency on bureaucratic red tape?

6. **Vendor philosophy.** How does the client view dealing with vendors? Do they have many long-term contacts with vendors? Are they loyal to their preferred suppliers? How closely integrated do they get with their best suppliers? Do they tend to buy on price or service? How do they view your industry? Do they see it as a necessary evil or as a value-added opportunity?

7. **Performance criteria.** How specific is the potential partner with regard to performance standards? Will they want you to sign service contracts? Will the reaction to non-performance be punitive? Are you capable of meeting stringent performance criteria?

8. **Key players.** Who are the key players? Are they people that you would enjoy working with? What are their business philosophies? Are these similar to yours?

9. **Relationships.** How is your relationship with the potential partner? Is it a long-term one? Have you worked well together? Has there been a history of give and take? Do they see you as a leader in your field? Do they value the relationship as it now exists? What partnerships have they formed with other suppliers? How successful have those been? Favourable answers to most of these questions would suggest that you have a basis for creating a partnership agreement.

Developing a Strategy

You cannot antagonize and influence at the same time.

UNKNOWN

Developing a long-term relationship with a client is challenging and difficult and rewarding. It evolves out of a conscious process.

Key steps in creating a strategic alliance with a client include these:

- making the decision to change the nature of relationships with customers
- identifying ideal partners
- researching the potential partner's organization
- formalizing the relationship
- organizing for success
- managing the ongoing relationship

Let's look at each one of these stages:

1. Making the decision to change the nature of relationships with customers

This change in direction could be prompted by

- reduced market share
- a rise in claims and returns
- mounting complaints
- high turnover of clients
- a proactive new strategy

2. Identifying ideal partners

With a decision made to get closer to the customer and build long-term partnerships, you should "pilot" your new approach with a small select number of clients before adopting this approach universally. Ideal partners would be organizations that

- see price as only one factor when making buying decisions
- can benefit from ongoing support after the sale
- provide you with a significant portion of their business
- would find it difficult to switch suppliers without incurring significant costs and disruption
- see you not as a necessary nuisance but as a valuable resource

3. Researching the potential partner's organization

This is a must. The information gathered will enable you to create a secure, long-term relationship.

4. Formalizing the relationship

Documentation of what each party will do to preserve the relationship is required. This could be a contract or letter of understanding. This understanding will cover

- key deliverables
- pricing
- joint marketing plans
- definition of points of contact
- mechanisms of how the relationship will be managed on a day-to-day basis

5. Organizing for success

Most organizations are inadequately structured for managing partnerships with clients. Implementing the following practices will ensure that an organization is structured effectively.

- Create a team to manage the relationship. The team would be an interdisciplinary group comprising people from all aspects of the organization.
- Document the processes that are key to an effective relationship.
- Streamline the important processes between the organization and clients.
- Empower people in the team to make decisions that will ensure the minimum of bureaucracy.
- Treat the team well, since their morale will have a huge impact on the ongoing relationship with the client.
- Restructure people into teams that focus on the customer, not on a function. Having interdisciplinary teams that "own" an entire process is far better than having to deal with multiple, competing organizational silos.
- Change the mindset of everyone from
  - "obtain customers" to "retain customers"
  - short-term sales to long-term relationships
  - minimal service to top-quality service
  - "that's not my responsibility" to "how can I help?"
- Change the performance management system so that rewards are based on process results, not short-term sales, and key indicators of the relationship are tracked and shared with all stakeholders.

6. Managing the ongoing relationship

Managing for the long term will include

* holding ongoing meetings with the client to review and continuously improve relationships
* making constant creative improvements that will delight and impress the client
* looking out for new opportunities to assist the client with additional services not originally considered.

The more effective you are, the easier it will be to expand the relationship and the volume of business.

Creating a Seamless
Electronic Supply Chain

*Strategic planning is worthless – unless
there is first a strategic vision.*

JOHN NAISBITT, AMERICAN BUSINESS WRITER

Technological advances are enabling all parties in a supply chain to
collaborate in ways that will dramatically improve margins, reduce costs
of supply and inventory, and ensure a higher level of availability of
inventory for the consumer. As part of the business-to-business (B2B)
explosion, more and more organizations are using electronic tools to
create a collaborative planning, forecasting, and replenishment system
that enables all partners — vendors, customers, and employees — to
build value and a competitive edge.

1. Most supply chains are inefficient. They are characterized by
- short-term arrangements between supplier and buyer
- suspicion
- ongoing negotiations based on price
- secrecy
- passing on of blame for ongoing problems

- high costs
- high levels of expediting

2. Electronic Assisted Sales Integration (EASI) is an attempt to establish a partnership that binds both parties to integrate their operations electronically and organizationally, and create a seamless service for the customer. The benefits of working together are
   - higher sales
   - lower inventory levels
   - higher availability to the customer
   - reduced lead times
   - reduced need for dealing with high-cost exceptions

3. Operating the system, once operational, is made easy with sophisticated electronic tools. For example, if the forecast of inventory needed at retail differs significantly from that which the producer is making, then the system would trigger an e-mail to both parties alerting them to the potential problem. Both parties would connect immediately, and resolve the discrepancy quickly. The communications could be done in any number of ways, including having a virtual meeting and using a whiteboard to brainstorm for solutions. Electronic integration will also promote automated ordering of inventories, thus eliminating human errors. For example, in a machine-to-machine (M2M) e-commerce environment, a company's computer would order goods from its supplier/partner when inventories run low.

4. The relationship is based on
   - a win-win approach
   - the sharing of information
   - joint planning

- joint goal-setting
- simultaneous execution of activities
- measurement of performance
- proactive problem solving
- celebration of successes

5. The primary advantages of EASI are that it
   - removes most of the uncertainty in the supply chain
   - creates seamless processes that reduce cost and waste
   - creates mechanisms to highlight problems in advance
   - provides tools to ensure that the "problems" are headed off

6. The primary obstacles to taking advantage of this new approach are
   - a combative culture based on suspicion rather than a collaborative one based on trust
   - an unwillingness to see these strategies as a key to survival and growth
   - unwillingness to share sensitive data for fear that it will be used against the organization
   - treatment of the change as a pilot to be terminated if results do not meet expectations. A pilot approach is sound only if one is determined to learn from it and continually improve an expanding number of partnerships.

7. Key measures of success are
   - increased sales
   - reduced inventories
   - fewer exceptions, expediting, and costs

8. A collaborative electronic system is best established in the following phases:
   - Appoint someone to champion the new initiative. This needs

to be someone senior who has the power to make changes and establish contractual relationships fairly quickly.

- Negotiate an agreement in principle, setting out the broad framework and goals.
- Create a project team comprised of all stakeholders. A consultant may be useful, especially if they have been successful in facilitating similar relationships elsewhere.
- Pick the software system and vendor that will customize a solution for you. Someone capable of supplying an integrated, turnkey solution is preferable to buying pieces of the puzzle from a variety of vendors. Latest, state-of-the-art systems include
  - person-to-person (P2P) document sharing, outside of the Internet
  - voice conferencing
  - active whiteboards for team communications, including problem solving and decision making
  - instant e-messaging for both hand-helds and wireless devices
- Develop a joint plan to manage the process collaboratively.
- Pick a pilot project. Test the newly created system with one product so that lessons can be learned and improvements made before expanding the process to other products.
- Forecast sales together. Identify exceptions to the forecast. Find root causes and work to eliminate them so that forecasting by both parties increases in accuracy.
- Forecast orders together. Identify exceptions. Find root causes and seek to prevent them from happening again.
- Generate orders.
- Fulfill orders.

9. Monitor and evaluate the partnership on an ongoing basis.

A Team Approach

A mile walked with a friend has only one hundred steps.

UNKNOWN

A strategic partnership with a client is too difficult and important to be handled by one person or a single department. A team of people who together add value to the relationship should manage the relationship. Creating such a team is not the function of a salesperson; it is the duty of senior management.

Here are some pointers to establish and maintain a successful service team:

1. Study the existing system to find flaws. Most organizations have cumbersome, inefficient work processes. Waste, duplication, and delays are everywhere. To identify these issues, identify key processes that impact on customers.
   - Document them on a process flow diagram.
   - Identify all the inefficiencies, including delays and duplication.
   - Look for ways of improving the process *dramatically*. Do this through a combination of brainstorming for new ideas,

identifying new technologies, and making organizational changes. Benchmark your approach against that of industry leaders to identify additional improved practices.

- Redesign the process. Document it. Get agreement on the new, streamlined process.
- Evaluate who needs to be a key player in the redesigned process.

2. Create a service team to implement and sustain the new client-focused process. The new team will comprise people who

- represent all key areas of the process (sales, engineering, information technology, production, distribution)
- are customer-driven
- will make the time to excel (none of us has the time to be on a new team, but some people will make the time)
- have the *power* to make changes

3. Design the team to promote their success. The team should have the following key ingredients:

- *Goals*. The team should define its direction with goals that are SMART:
    - **S** pecific
    - **M** easurable
    - **A** greed upon by all members
    - **R** ealistic
    - **T** ime-based
- *Standards of performance*. The team should set minimum standards of performance for such things as
    - response times
    - quality levels
    - behaviour

- *Structure.* Roles, including leadership, should be clearly
  defined. Reward systems, preferably promoting teamwork as
  opposed to individual achievements, should also be defined.
- *A sense of belonging.* The team should, if possible,
  - co-locate
  - meet regularly
  - choose a name to give them a feeling of togetherness

  The team should also create a mission statement that clearly
  defines *what* it does, *who* it will serve, *how* it will do so, and
  why it will do so (the benefits for the organization and team
  members).

4. Unite the team with the client's team. The teams should meet
   with the purpose of capitalizing on the opportunities for mutual
   benefits. The first meeting should be devoted to
   - getting to know one another
   - sharing a common vision
   - identifying obstacles to success
   - creating plans to overcome the obstacles
   - deciding on key measures of success
   - setting up a structure to enable ongoing problem solving
     and decision making that will encourage continuous
     improvements and innovations

5. Ongoing meetings should be devoted to
   - reviewing and celebrating successes
   - solving problems
   - exploring new opportunities

A Test of Effectiveness

Complete the questionnaire below to assess the strength of your relationship with key clients.

Choose **1** if you disagree totally
       2 if you disagree somewhat
       3 if you neither agree or disagree
       4 if you agree somewhat
       5 if you agree totally

1. Our organization has a conscious, documented policy of developing strategic partnerships with key clients. **1 2 3 4 5**

2. We have a plan (step-by-step process) to convert clients into strategic partnerships. **1 2 3 4 5**

3. We study the businesses of our major clients to identify their business strategy so that we can integrate our efforts with theirs. **1 2 3 4 5**

4. We seek ways to move from potentially
adversarial relationships with clients to a
relationship of interdependence.   1 2 3 4 5

5. Our whole organization is involved in the
service of clients.   1 2 3 4 5

6. We have structured our organization into
interdisciplinary teams to serve key clients.   1 2 3 4 5

7. We do not compete on price.   1 2 3 4 5

8. Most of our business is from long-term
relationships with selected business partners.   1 2 3 4 5

9. Our sales forecasts are made with our
business partners.   1 2 3 4 5

10. We meet regularly with business partners to
review our relationship and look for ways
to improve performance.   1 2 3 4 5

11. Our production schedules are made in
consultation with our business partners.   1 2 3 4 5

12. We have integrated our information systems
to share information with clients and vendors.   1 2 3 4 5

13. We meet regularly with our clients to deal with
problems and find new ways to enhance
our relationship.   1 2 3 4 5

14. We try to exceed the expectations of our
clients, not just meet them.   **1 2 3 4 5**

15. Our reward systems place an emphasis on
service by teams rather than individuals.   **1 2 3 4 5**

16. We measure the effectiveness of our
customer service.   **1 2 3 4 5**

17. We regularly review the effectiveness of our
customer service to find new methods
of improvement.   **1 2 3 4 5**

TOTAL YOUR SCORE =

KEY TO INTERPRETATION:

*If you scored 18–36, you have a weak relationship with clients.
You need to improve soon, or you won't have any relationships.
If you scored 37–72, you have a mediocre relationship with clients.
Unless they are very loyal, they may move on to other partnerships.
If you scored 73–90, you have a strong relationship with clients.
Your clients will endeavour to partner with you.*

9

Technology

Using the
Latest Technologies

Science and technology multiply around us. To an increasing extent they dictate the languages in which we speak and think. Either we use the languages, or we remain mute.

J.G. BALLARD, BRITISH AUTHOR

As a sales rep, you need to be organized, able to communicate, able to find contact information quickly, and able to remember little tidbits about each of your customers. New technologies can help you with all of the above. Here is the approach you should take, as well as the tools that will help you do your job effectively:

1. Start soon. Having said that, there are two advantages to delaying:
   - The cost of new hardware is declining rapidly.
   - New software is becoming more simple and powerful.

   But none of these advantages outweighs the problems associated with not being able to take advantage of the astonishing technological tools that can make you more efficient and effective.

2. Don't be overwhelmed. You can't learn all there is to know overnight. Moreover, technology is constantly evolving, and it's impossible to fully keep up. Just do your best to keep your knowledge and tools current.

3. Don't buy any equipment on the advice of a salesperson. Ask people you trust about hardware, software, and vendors that they have found to offer good service and fair prices. Price is secondary when it comes to hardware since the services that come with the product, such as 24/7 access to a toll-free help line, will be invaluable to a new user.

4. Don't buy more software than you will be able to master in the short term, unless it is part of a bundle of products.

5. Prepare yourself for some frustration. Learning new tools and changing the way you do things will be exasperating. There will also be times of exhilaration as your new tools start to work for you.

6. Find a coach, someone who cares enough to spend time with you. Such a person need not be a tech wiz but should be able to explain technical information in simple language that even a child can understand.

7. Offer your coach an incentive to teach you. It can be a financial reward, or an opportunity for you to share your non-technical skills in return.

8. Set a goal for yourself. Identify the most useful tools and prioritize their usefulness in terms of your job. Aim to become proficient in one tool at a time. If it is a computer, break down the goal into mini-goals, such as learning how to navigate the operating system, then word processing, then learning a time-management system, and so on.

9. After you have finished each module, or mastered one tool, celebrate your success immediately. Also, ensure that you continue to use that tool so that your learning stays with you.

10. If you are learning to use a computer, create your own "help line" folder on your desktop. In it, describe all the little "tricks" you have learned that will be useful to you in the future, but which you might otherwise forget.

11. Learn in a way that best suits your preferred learning style. Are you self-directed or do you prefer structure and help? The more self-directed you are, the easier it will be to learn, as you will be able to work on your own through Internet-based programs, CD-ROMs, or manuals. If, however, you prefer the human touch, consider signing up for in-house programs or for night school courses that offer the flexibility of working at your own pace.

12. Personal Information Management Systems (PIMS) are software programs that allow you to build a database of customers. There are many outstanding PIMS on the market, including AVT, Maximizer, Access, and Outlook. With the most effective of these, you can customize your database any way you want. Especially useful is the grouping option, which allows you to group your clients into specific categories, such as type of retail store. With PIMS you can

- keep notes on each customer and their trading history.
- extract specific information quickly, including not only clients' contact information and account history, but also information such as their hobbies, their birth dates, and the names and ages of their kids that allows you to give your communications with them a personal touch.

Aside from their obvious use as databases, PIMS also typically come with the following features:

- to-do lists (including priority options)
- calendars
- a reminder function
- e-mail capability

13. The following products are currently the most popular:

- *Desktop computers* are incredibly powerful and allow you to do a host of things, such that your whole office can be run on a single machine that costs you a little more than $1000.
- *Laptop computers,* which typically weigh 4–7 pounds, can fit into a briefcase and be used for everything that a desktop can. They typically have a little less power than a desktop, and cost about twice as much.
- *Handheld organizers.* The latest Palms, Handsprings, and Blackberrys allow you to connect to e-mail, the Global Positioning System, the Web, and more! They can synchronize with your office computer's database, so you can work on the road without lugging around a laptop.
- *Digital cameras* allow you to take pictures of displays, the competitions' products, and the like. You can then show them to key people in your organization.

- *Cell phones* are a wonderful tool for salespeople to confirm appointments, let people know if you are running late, check for messages, and return calls quickly. But these portable telephones can do much more. Today, they can surf the Net and send and receive e-mails. Some cell services allow you to use your phone across North America, while others have a global reach.

14. There will be a proliferation of cell phones and other wireless devices to access the Internet in the next few years as the demand to stay connected increases exponentially. But wireless Internet technology is in its infancy, so depending on your needs and location you could find the device you buy about as useful as a periscope in a mine shaft. Deciding which device to buy is tricky, to say the least. But, consider these factors when making your decision:
   - *Speed.* How long will it take to download your favourite Web sites and your e-mail? Some devices are currently so slow that one might suffer rigor mortis while waiting. This problem will be addressed as newer high-speed technologies replace the current operating systems. Generally, devices made specifically for wireless Internet access operate better than those that are multifunctional.
   - *Coverage.* Many services operate well in major metropolitan areas, but fail to offer access in smaller cities.

15. Make use of the many free services that the Internet offers. There are a growing number of applications and services that salespeople can access on the Internet. They include the following:
   - *Fax retrieval.* Services such as www.j2.com offer you the ability to retrieve your compressed fax and voice mails in your own e-mail box.

- *Web site hosting.* www.freeservers.com will allow you to choose a site name, build a site, and host up to 20 MB for free. Freeservers will also process the e-mails sent to your domain (if you have one), either by forwarding them to the account you specify or storing them.
- *Web site registration.* www.namedemo.com and www.namezero.com both provide free registration of domain names.
- *Acting as your storefront.* www.freemerchant.com will give you a free storefront that carries your domain name as a sub-domain in the Web address (cy@askcharney.freemerchant.com is an example). The service will provide you with the tools to conduct credit card transactions, hold auctions, track shipments, and log Web traffic.
- *Having your own intranet.* This facility will allow you to enhance communications by allowing people you choose to share files and schedule meetings. www.intranet.com will allow you to create an intranet for free, permitting anyone with a password — such as your staff, associates, and customers — to access the information.
- *Telephone calls.* You can make free calls across the United States using www.net2phone.com.

16. Free sites on the Internet do have a downside. Here are some disadvantages:
    - *Enormous downloads.* Many of these free sites will take up large amounts of hard drive space. They also take ages to download, especially if you're doing so over a phone line.
    - *Lack of longevity.* The dot-com business is unpredictable and in its infancy. Portals that you may rely on can disappear overnight.

- *Annoying and obtrusive advertisements.* Most free sites generate income from advertising. So, expect some temporary annoyance when your e-mail gets covered up with an advertisement.
- *Unwanted e-mails.* Not all sites are ethical. They may give your e-mail number to Internet marketers who, in spite of your best efforts, will probably not remove your number from their lists. So, expect a daily slew of annoying mail.

Electronic
Communications

*The more elaborate our means of communication,
the less we communicate.*

JOSEPH PRIESTLEY (1733–1804), ENGLISH THEOLOGIAN AND SCIENTIST

*C*ommunicating by e-mail can be the best and fastest method of communicating with your clients. It will also be the cheapest, enabling you to reduce time and costs associated with the phone. Modern wireless technology will also enable to you to send and receive e-mails from anywhere that you are able to use a cell phone.

Anyone relying on a phone to make appointments or do follow-up for decisions will be increasingly frustrated by the difficulties associated with getting the right person on the phone. Today, most people have and use call answering or screening to avoid conversations that are not a priority. Many people simply do not return phone calls, period. If they do, the chances of you being on the other end of the phone, waiting for the call, are slim indeed.

But most people respond fairly quickly to e-mails. So, improve your e-mail communications by using these strategies:

1. Avoid "spamming" clients. People really resent their e-mail
system being clogged up with unwanted and unnecessary
messages. If you need to send out general information to clients,
then send it to people who know you, ask for their permission,
in advance, and give them a process to be excluded from any
future mailings, should they so choose.

2. Send bulk mail sparingly. Ensure that the content is something
your audience would appreciate.

3. Create a short message with a title that clearly describes why the
receiver needs to read on.

4. If you feel that the best way to contact potential clients is through
unsolicited e-mails, look for a list that covers your potential client
base best. Before buying into the process, consider doing a test
with a sample of the addresses so that you can gauge the potential
value of a mass e-mailing.

Using the Internet
for Research

*Basic research is what I am doing when
I don't know what I'm doing.*

WERNHER VON BRAUN (1912–77), GERMAN-AMERICAN ENGINEER

The Internet is a wonderful tool that will allow you to research such things as the details of potential clients, people/organizations to network with, and new complementary products and services, to name a few. Here's how to do it effectively.

1. If you want to check out a company's URL that has been sent to you in an e-mail, you can locate it simply by clicking on it.

2. If you want to look up something without having a URL, you can easily do so by using your favourite search engine. Enter key words and hit your enter key.

3. If you get too many hits, or if most have little to do with your chosen topic, consider narrowing your search by linking words with a plus sign. This will force the search engine to be more discriminating and offer you a more limited choice.

192 ▲ USING THE INTERNET FOR RESEARCH

4. Access large amounts of data quickly using the Internet. You can download information, take what you want, and copy and paste only those parts that are of interest to you.

5. Being a good Web surfer requires discipline. The Web is full of distractions that can cause you to veer off in a multitude of directions, wasting precious time. Avoid time wastage, particularly during company time, by not clicking on "booby traps" that are aiming to lure you to more enticing pursuits.

6. Avoid the lure of chat rooms. There are thousands of chat rooms on subjects of all description. To benefit from them, consider joining one or more that relate to your industry or profession. You can learn a lot from people around the world, and share your wisdom at the same time, too.

Creating a Web Page

. . . very soon everyone on earth will have 15 Megabytes of fame.

M.G. SIRIAM

A Web page is your electronic brochure, available to the world. It will help you create an image that can be as favourable and impressive as the largest organization's, even though they may have fancy offices in a downtown high-rise and you're operating in the basement of your home. So, how you set up your Web site and how you use it will have a measurable impact on its effectiveness.

1. Getting started on the Internet is probably best done by using an expert. It will make the process much quicker and less frustrating. Deciding on whether to go it alone or use an expert should be based on a cost-benefit analysis pitting the cost of your time against the cost of an expert.

- Today, experts don't need to cost the earth. You'll find an endless number of Web page designers in your local newspaper, Yellow Pages, local community college, or among your neighbourhood school kids. The latter will be most cost-effective, but often prove to be unreliable.

- To get started you will need a computer. You will need a PC, hand-held, or laptop. The PC is the cheapest, but offers least flexibility from a portability perspective. As a minimum, you'll probably want a computer with
  - a Pentium III microchip to be able to process more sophisticated data and 3-D diagrams;
  - a 56K modem, to ensure a reasonable speed in transferring data to and from the Internet;
  - 700 MHz to process information quickly; and
  - 128 megabytes of RAM to be able to use more than one software program simultaneously.

2. Whe choosing a Web address (URL), bear these principles in mind:
  - Pick something that people will be able to remember. Associate the URL designation with your name. For example if your company is Only Sox Inc., then consider www.onlysox.com.
  - Short is always better. A long URL will invariably lead people to making mistakes when they are trying to access your Web page, causing concern about whether your URL is operational or not.
  - Choose a "first-tier" address such as a dot-com, dot-net, or dot-org. It projects an image of universality. A second-tier URL, such as dot-on.ca, lets the user know that you operate more locally, which in some cases may be an advantage, but in others is less prestigious.
  - An easy way to find a name that you can use is to check with a registry, such as domainpeople.com. If your chosen name is available, you can immediately reserve it for whatever period you want, for a fee.

3. You will need a Web browser, such as Netscape or Microsoft's Internet Explorer.

Learn to use one of the software programs, such as Microsoft's FrontPage or Adobe's PageMill, so that you can update your Web page very quickly as often as is necessary. These programs avoid the necessity of learning to use HTML and other programming languages, which can be intimidating.

4. Use a reliable service-oriented Internet provider. An ideal provider is one that offers
   - 24/7 service
   - patient, knowledgeable people on their help desk
   - high-speed access
   - ability to log in from any major centre worldwide

5. Design your Web page with these criteria in mind:
   - The front page is bright, simple, eye-catching, and uncluttered.
   - Text is written in simple, bold letters, which are easy to read. Fancy texts are sometimes difficult to read on a computer screen.
   - The colour is the same as your stationery so that it maintains your corporate image.
   - The front page creates an immediate favourable impression. It should contain
     - your logo
     - a short crisp message letting people know what you are all about
     - links to other parts of your site, typically in tabs on the left hand side of the page

- links to other useful URLs
- It should be easy to contact you.

6. Encourage people to contact you by registering with you.
Create a way to make the process fun and simple by
- asking a few basic questions such as name, title, organization, and e-mail address. A phone number would be useful, but may bring about resistance, as people might feel that you will be badgering them.
- limiting the length of the questionnaire to a few lines that require short simple answers
- highlighting the submit button, so that it is easy to see and use
- offering some kind of reward for responding, such as a free catalogue, sample, or consultation. Some kind of draw for a prize might sweeten the pot and encourage a larger response.

Using the Internet
to Promote Sales

The Internet is a business accelerator unlike anything seen before. It has a scalpel-like propensity to slice away activities, processes, and institutions that do not add value to customers.

ED MCMAHON, *BRICKS TO CLICKS: E-STRATEGIES THAT WILL ENHANCE YOUR BUSINESS*

The cost of entering the Internet is low. It is inconceivable today that one can ignore the Internet as a way of sharing information, promoting yourself and your products, displaying your products, and taking orders. Sales on the Internet are increasing exponentially. As more people look to the Internet as their preferred method of transacting business, so does the pressure increase for you to have a presence in cyberspace.

The Internet can open your world globally overnight. Moreover, an attractive site builds consumer confidence and presents you as a more legitimate enterprise.

Use the Internet to create new interest in what you have to offer and to manage existing sales. But never expect your Web page to replace the personal touch. A wise salesperson will know which clients need the soft touch and which need the high-tech approach.

1. A Web site will give you many advantages. It will help you to
- exchange information quickly
- reduce your cost of advertising literature, phone calls, and postage
- enable people who don't want a sales presentation to conduct some low-risk research of their own, prior to committing to a one-on-one discussion
- pre-qualify prospects, allowing you to focus on those that are most interested

2. Maintain interest in your Web page by
- updating it regularly, as frequently as every two weeks
- listing new products, current research results, new people, industry trends, and the latest innovations
- making it fun to explore by adding such things as tips, questions and answers, appropriate jokes, and quotes by people of great wisdom

3. Attract as many people to your site as possible by
- registering with as many search engines as possible, particularly the most popular ones such as Yahoo, Lycos, Infoseek, and Google
- showing your URL on all company literature, premises, and even vehicles

4. While ensuring that your information is comprehensive, be cautious about including trade secrets and areas that give you a competitive advantage. You can be sure that your competitors will visit your Web site and learn from it in an attempt to reduce any competitive advantage that you may have.

10
Career Effectiveness

Goal Setting

A good goal is like a strenuous exercise – it makes you stretch.

MARY KAY ASH, CHAIRMAN, MARY KAY COSMETICS

Selling is a process of setting goals and achieving them. People in sales are probably better than most at setting goals. You are constantly budgeting sales and comparing actual against budget. But goal setting often slips when it comes to ourselves.

You will enhance your career and effectiveness by focusing on yearly, monthly, weekly, and even daily goals. Your goals are your roadmap to a successful future. They will determine the direction in which you are headed and ensure that you reach your destination. Here's how to set goals:

1. Create your personal vision of where you see yourself five to ten years ahead. Don't be modest. Picture yourself as being highly successful. Then imagine your success described as a newspaper headline. Create that headline and superimpose it on a newspaper. Then copy it and post it on your wall next to your mission so that you never forget what you need to do daily (mission) and where you are headed (vision).

2. To achieve your goals you have to know exactly what they are. Make sure they are challenging and SMART:

- **S** pecific. "I want to be the top-selling rep in the company" is much better than, "I want to improve this year."
- **M** easurable. "I want to sell 20% more than I did last year."
- **A** greed upon
- **R** ealistic
- **T** ime-based

3. Write your goals down. Post them in a spot where you can see them. Refer to them for motivation.

4. Make sure your goals do not conflict with your fundamental values. There's no point planning to make a fortune if you are happy with what you have or if you are leery about exploiting others on the way to the top.

5. Put your goals in order of importance. At the top of the list go the goals that satisfy a personal need. Do these things first. If you want to spend more time with your family, arrange your schedule to enable you to do so. You can't wait for your schedule to arrange itself.

6. Formulate a plan. What do you need to do tomorrow? next month? next year? Once you have a long-range plan, you can stop worrying about next year and apply yourself to the task at hand.

7. Check your plan regularly. Have you met your monthly goals? And are they taking you where you want to go? If not, now is the time to reformulate them.

8. Look at your goals often to see if you're on track.

9. Once you've set goals, make a list of roadblocks that are standing in your way. Ignore those that are unlikely to happen. With the balance, highlight those that you have control over. Develop a plan to solve them one at a time. For example, you might consider a lack of training as a roadblock. So, develop a plan to get some training through your preferred learning method — reading, self-study, computer-based training, or workshops.

10. Create a personal mission statement. Sign it and display it on your wall so that you constantly remind yourself of what you need to do daily in order to be successful. To create a mission statement, complete the blank portions of the template (see Diagram 1 on the next page).

Here is an example:

"I, Samantha Smart, provide timely, reliable, courteous advice to doctors and other medical professionals in Toronto in order to improve the market penetration of Better Medications products and to ensure that my career will be fulfilling and fun."

DIAGRAM 1: TEMPLATE FOR CREATING A PERSONAL MISSION STATEMENT

WHO _____
(Name)

WHAT _____
(State what you do)

HOW _____
(State how you do it)

FOR _____
(Describe your customer)

WHERE _____
(Describe the geographical area you cover)

WHY _____
(Describe the benefits to yourself and your organization)

11. Anticipate and remove roadblocks. What kinds of challenges will you face? Make a list of them. The larger the potential sale, the more formal you would want to be. This being the case, consider documenting them using a force-field analysis (see diagram on the next page).

12. Don't let yourself off the hook. Tell people what your goals are. Then, when you feel like slacking off, other people's expectations will keep you going.

FORCE FIELD ANALYSIS							
Goal							
←		Roadblocks		**Positive Forces**		→	
#	Item	P	C	#	Item	P	C

13. Ask yourself the hard questions. Do you really want the thing you've set out to do? Or is it a way to defer doing something else?

14. Harness your mental power. Can you envision success? Can you see yourself achieving your goal? This is how professional athletes take their performance to the next level.

15. Don't become obsessed. The line between being driven and being monomaniacal should never be crossed. Your personal life, and quite possibly your health, will suffer.

16. Keep moving. Daydreaming will never get you where you want to go. What you need is action. You don't have to do it all at once, however. After all, you don't want the sort of thing that just falls into your lap. But if you make strides every day, you'll get where you want to be.

17. Don't beat yourself up when you stumble. And when you succeed, reward yourself.

Career Choices

Too bad that all the people who know how to run this country are busy driving taxis and cutting hair.

GEORGE BURNS (1896–1996), AMERICAN COMEDIAN

We all know it — the world has changed. Markets are global. Companies are downsizing and outsourcing. New strategic partnerships are also changing the nature of the sales process, requiring less knocking on doors and more management of relationships. This calls for fewer salespeople and more account managers and sales executives.

How are you going to position yourself in this new environment? The skill set of the new salesperson is a far cry from the old. Planning for your new role is important. There are many issues to consider as you contemplate your future either within your organization or in a new one.

1. While you rediscover yourself, ask yourself these questions:
- **"What am I all about?"**
  That is, what do you respect in yourself and in others? These are the things like honesty, integrity, decency, and congeniality — values that, if ignored, will sap your enthusiasm for your company and perhaps for your career. Write them down. Do you

meet your own standards day-to-day? Will a prospective
employer measure up to these expectations?

- **"What am I capable of?"**
Do you have any skills that set you apart from others in the
market? Keep track of your skills as you acquire them and put
them into practice. Now, what sort of company would be looking
for someone with just those skills? Do you want to be pushed to
your limits? What gets you excited? What is going to make you
want to work long hours?

- **"What kind of price am I willing to pay for a career
change?"**
Are you flexible? Are you willing to take risks? This is serious stuff.
Consider the possibilities: the new job might not work out or you
might be unemployed for a while. So now is the time to ask
yourself whether whatever it is you're looking for in a new career
might not be available where you are right now. Let's face it.
Changing jobs can be frustrating. But if you are resilient and
adaptable, you should be just fine.

2. To determine whether or not you could get what you need where
you are right now, you need to decide exactly what you want.
- First, figure out what you like about your current situation.
Make a list. Do you like
  - your co-workers?
  - the challenge?
  - the autonomy?
  If you are considering a career move, this list may be short.
  Be fair.
- Now, make a list of the things you expect from your dream job.
  - What would you be doing?
  - Where would you be doing it? What is the environment like?

- Who would you be working with?
- How big or small is the company?
- The next step is to put the two lists side by side. Now you can quantify the urgency of your move. What appears on the "ideal" list that is missing from the "real" list? How important is the missing piece?
- Make a list of the most important elements missing from the "real" list. Keep this master list handy. This list will guide your upcoming decisions.

3. It's time to start looking around. Look first at your own organization. Are there positions within the company that would meet your expectations? Perhaps you don't have to leave after all. If you do, begin researching other organizations. What are you looking for? A position that meets the "master-list" criteria from step 2.

4. Once you've done this, and it could take a while, decide what your ideal position is and what your backup choice would be. Now evaluate each, keeping in mind that if neither makes the grade, you may be better off where you are. Here's what to consider:
- *Potential hurdles.* Would you need specific training, for example? Are you sufficiently familiar with your proposed field?
- *Steps to get over these hurdles.* Are there courses you could take? seminars you could attend? Do you know people in this new field? Make a tentative plan.
- *The pros and cons of the new position.* Weigh them carefully.
- *The worst-case scenario.* Change can be difficult. Are you ready?
- *The best-case scenario.* This should give you the courage to make your move.

5. Ultimately, your research and networking should result in a job offer. But how do you know whether to accept it? Make a list of the things you're looking for:

- salary
- benefits
- hours
- location
- everything you determined in step 2!

6. Don't overlook good advice. Talk it over. Bounce your ideas around with

- someone you can trust
- someone in neither your new or your old organization
- someone who knows what he or she is talking about, that is, someone who has made a career change
- a career counsellor who can test your suitability for this or that field and guide you more objectively than you can yourself

Getting Ahead

*Mama exhorted her children at every opportunity to "jump at de sun."
We might not land on the sun, but at least we would
get off the ground.*

ZORA NEALE HURSTON (1903–60), AMERICAN DRAMATIST

Aiming to be Vice President of Marketing or Sales? Moving up the ladder doesn't happen by chance. It happens because of the choices you make. And waiting for something good to happen is *choosing* to do nothing. You would never explicitly choose that, would you? You have to take the bull by the horns if you want a promotion. Above all, always be assertive. Let your goals be known. Ask for promotions and opportunities whenever it seems appropriate. Here's how to get yourself in the right position to make that move.

1. Take every opportunity to prove yourself. This means giving everything you've got.
   - Have the best attitude in the organization. Always be positive. And always be passionate about the organization, its people, and its products.
   - Take on as much responsibility and authority as you can and

rise to the occasion. You may have to push yourself, but ultimately you'll prove yourself worthy of the new roles.

- Use the freedom you have in sales. Do things in your own time that will get back to the company, reflecting well on your commitment to the organization.
- Do more than your job description requires. And keep a record of all you've done. Present these records at your next performance review. These new endeavours will be added to your job description. With a greater role comes greater recognition. You'll be on your way up.
- Lead by example in collaborative work. Give it your all and your team will follow your lead.
- Step forward when others step back. Do that extra job; volunteer for that task force.
- Share your strengths. Teach others. For one thing, you'll learn from the experience. For another, you'll be seen as competent and forward thinking.

2. Have a strategy.
- Make a five-year plan. What do you have to do to get where you want? What stands in your way? Make a list of the obstacles and the things you have to do to get around them. Talk to your boss about how to achieve these milestones.
- Track your progress according to the milestones you've set for yourself. Adjust your sights if things have gone astray or changed along the way. Always be moving in the direction you want to go.
- Stay away from the conflicts that divide any office. There is no way to win these battles, and lots of ways to lose. But if you are going to be drawn in, make sure you pick the winner.
- Don't lose sight of the forest because you're staring at the trees

all day. Look for trends and patterns. That way you'll know an opportunity when you see one.

- Never rest on your laurels or stop learning. Keep taking courses. Share your knowledge with others. And ask others to share knowledge with you.
- Don't rely on your own self-evaluation. Look for feedback. Ask some important people how you are doing — and don't argue with them if you hear something you don't like. Just fix it.
- Don't get emotional. This is part of a long-term plan.
- Remember, even if what you hear is criticism, there is advice hidden in there somewhere.
- Defend yourself only if your critic has got something dead wrong. Keep in mind that anything you say in your defence will sound like you have lost objectivity.
- Thank the person for the observations — whether you agree or not.
- Learn from negative experiences. If you're fired or demoted, don't feel sorry for yourself or blame others. Figure out what went wrong. Then never do it again.

3. Surround yourself with people who are on your side.
- Watch your boss. What are her priorities? Your boss wants to look good, just as you do. Help her out, and sooner or later your boss will do the same for you.
- Keep your boss's interests in mind. If there is a storm brewing, be the person to break the news to her. Your boss will appreciate the heads-up.
- Know what your boss expects of you. That way you'll never disappoint her by accident. And remember, if your achievements cannot be measured, they may not be perceived.
- Make sure your boss knows your goals. Talk about how she

feels things could work out and how you could go about
achieving them. Ask for feedback and advice.

- Don't be stingy. If you have sales tips and leads that can help
your colleagues, share them. Your peers will look up to you
and see you as a leader.
- Watch those who know what they're doing and those who have
accomplished those things you're striving for. Learn from them
and if possible ask someone you respect to be your mentor.
When you face difficult decisions, ask someone who has been
there before.
- Keep your word. And always deliver *more* than you promise.
- Look at things from others' perspectives. What do you look like
in the eyes of a client or customer? You may find that what you
want is in conflict with what they want. Look for balance and
you'll have a more productive relationship.
- Publicly thank those who have helped you. They will love you
for it. And they'll be eager to help you again.
- Find ways to be successful without stepping on toes. The more
people you turn into enemies, the more enemies you are likely
to meet down the road. Learn to be gracious.
- Don't think of your colleagues as enemies or competitors.
Put yourself in that role. You are the person who will make or
break your career, not them. If you are working against your
peers, you will find that they are working against you.
- Don't hide your ideas. If you have something to say, say it with
enthusiasm. Leaders are people who clearly believe in what
they are doing.

4. Become the person the company cannot live without.
- Make yourself the go-to person by grabbing opportunities to do
things others can't or won't. For example, you could be the

most technologically adept. Or the expert on outsourcing. And when there is a crisis, be the person taking up slack. People will count on you.

- Be an expert. If you do something remarkable (and you should), write an article about it. Show it to your boss and look for a suitable publisher. Your credentials are your ticket up the ladder.

- Make the organization's interests your own. Don't waste or misuse resources. Instead, look for ways to make the company more efficient.

5. A few other things:

- If you want to be a manager, dress like a manager. If you want to be VP, dress like one. Look like you belong where you want to be.

- Pick your battles. Don't take on projects that do not show your skills and knowledge to advantage. And avoid projects that are likely to eat up too much time and material.

- Avoid any unnecessary risk of failure — go where your chances of success are best.

- Don't sell yourself short by focusing attention on opportunities elsewhere. If the grass really is greener on the other side of the hill, go there. If not, buckle down and apply yourself where you are.

Ethical and
Moral Behaviour

Let unswerving integrity be your watchword.

BERNARD BARUCH (1870–1965), AMERICAN FINANCIER

$\mathcal{S}$alespeople provide a window into an organization. Their behaviour will be the yardstick by which to judge the organization. Conducting yourself in an ethical manner is not only the right thing to do; it's the only thing to do. It's a way of developing relationships that will yield handsome dividends in the long term.

Put another way, ethical behaviour will not only advance your career — it will improve your whole life. Here are some guidelines to help you do so.

1. Be honest. Don't be "creative" in documenting expenses. Avoid the temptation to accept bribes of any type. And, never offer an undue incentive to buy from your company other than tokens of appreciation such as a business lunch. Major gifts, such as free trips, are not only immoral, but illegal too and will surely get you fired — or worse. The short-term benefit will never offset the negative long-term damage to your career. And, it will put you onto a track of always finding a devious way to do things other than the right way.

2. Maintain confidentiality when asked to do so.

3. Be fair. Find a balance between your needs and those of others. Try to satisfy as many people as possible. That way, you will find that others will try to help you when necessary.

4. Be free of prejudice and bigotry — judge people on the basis of merit only. Prejudging situations and people will ensure that you set up artificial barriers with people who can assist you in one way or another.

5. Be loyal to your employer. Give them 100% effort. Represent them with dignity. Portray them positively in the marketplace, knowing that they, like any other organization, are probably less than perfect.

6. Carry your share of the workload. Pitch in and help others when needed, even when you are not asked to.

7. Don't misuse your organization's assets. Don't exaggerate expense accounts or use the company's assets, such as vehicles, for personal use. When there is a need to do so, get permission.

8. Don't moonlight. Salespeople have lots of freedom. This should never be used for personal gain such as selling for another organization.

9. Avoid cheating in sales contests. Sometimes salespeople might hold orders back to put them in the following month when a contest is run. It might cause late delivery. And it will deprive someone else of a prize richly deserved.

10. Tell the truth about your product or service. Never exaggerate the capability of your product. "Best" is a word that is bandied around, and is often expected. But suggesting a technical specification beyond that which will be delivered can result in a lawsuit for misrepresentation.

11. Never talk about someone who isn't around. And *never* insult an absent colleague or client. It will come back to haunt you.

12. Don't beat around the bush.
- If someone has performed poorly, let them know. Right away. If you're afraid of hurting someone's feelings, that's fine. But never avoid an issue to avoid wounding someone. You'll have to get to the point some time. Better it be now.
- If someone has offended you, take it up with that person — not the boss. He or she does not want to know. Stand your ground. Don't attack the person; address the behaviour.
- Don't get into situations where you have to keep secrets or maintain some sort of false impression.

13. Always be fair.
- Copyright is important. Don't take it lightly. Ideas are meant to be shared. Whole texts are not.
- Would you like to see someone take credit for your work? Of course not. Give people the credit they deserve and they will be happy to work with you again.

14. Be respected for your honesty.
- A false resumé is not only unethical, it may be illegal and it could cost you your job.
- Don't let your enthusiasm run away with your better judgement. If you are talking about facts, have data ready to support your argument. If not, remember: you are only sharing your opinion. Make sure that is clear to your listeners.

15. Put your organization in the best possible light. Does your company have a values statement? If so, it's your job to abide by it.

16. Don't betray your colleagues' trust by spying on them or blowing the whistle for little things. You won't get points from your boss for being a rat. Only step in if the law is being broken or the company's well-being is at stake.

17. Treat others as you wish to be treated. That means not embarrassing them — especially your boss. If you violate the chain of command, you are making your boss look bad. Share all memos that go above your boss or to another department.

18. Keep your word. Only promise what you can deliver. The benefits are manifold.
- You'll attract and impress other ethical people.
- You'll save all the time unscrupulous people waste avoiding the traps they've set for themselves and fixing the problems they've left scattered behind them.
- You'll gain momentum to take you forward to the next promise.

Professionalism

We make a living by what we get.
But we make a life by what we give.

WINSTON CHURCHILL (1874–1965), BRITISH PRIME MINISTER

Salespeople with longevity have and behave with professionalism. What does this mean and why should you do it? Consider yourself a real pro if you

1. Love problems! You see opportunities where others see roadblocks. You realize that your profession is not an easy one. You demonstrate that you are not an order-taker. You encounter obstacles all the time, but you systematically go about finding creative solutions that benefit the customer.

2. Have a sense of urgency. Get on things quickly. You hate to procrastinate. You return phone calls and e-mails quickly because modern technology enables this and you consider it important.

3. Are respectful of other people's time. When you attend meetings, you show up on time. You stay on track and stick to the agenda.

4. Serve your customers after the sale. You know that service starts after the sale is made. You follow up to ensure that the client's expectations have been met. And you call periodically if you have additional ideas about how the product or service can be used.

5. Dress appropriately. You realize that each industry has different expectations for dress. You know that your clothing sends a signal to others about who you are and how you view your customers. So, you

- Mirror the dress of your customers, or always choose to dress one level above. For example, if your customers tend to dress in jeans, you wear sports slacks. If they wear a blazer, you wear a suit.
- Don't wear lots of jewellery, which might suggest you are flaunting your success.
- Don't dress in a sexually provocative fashion. You're there to sell your product or service — not your body!

6. Go beyond what is expected. You are the talk of the town because you want to WOW! each client. And you see each encounter as an opportunity to test your creativity and enthusiasm, to be the best at what you do. You delight your customers with

- unusually speedy service
- an upgraded product at no additional cost
- unexpected ongoing advice
- better terms
- free training

Getting Things Done
Through Others

A spoonful of honey will catch more flies than a gallon of vinegar.

BENJAMIN FRANKLIN (1706–90), AMERICAN STATESMAN

*J*ust as others can't get their jobs done without you, you wouldn't get far without others. Getting your colleagues onside is absolutely essential to moving forward, whether you have an ambitious new project or a minor change to make. Here are a few strategies to help you get everyone on the same page.

1. Don't pretend you're a lone wolf. Letting others know you rely on them is the first step towards collaboration.

2. Treat others the way you would like to be treated. You want respect, dignity, and consideration? Then that's what you should offer others.

3. Don't look down on those below you in rank. If you abuse power, expect it to be abused against you later. More importantly, abuse of power will only squander the trust and respect you've been trying to develop.

4. Keep the tone in the work environment positive. The more pumped everybody is, the more you'll accomplish.

5. Don't "call for mommy." If a colleague has done something you don't appreciate, take the issue up with that person — not your boss. You have to be able to work with people without the threat of the boss behind you. And your boss won't like it either.

6. Engage in give-and-take. Do favours whenever the opportunity presents itself. One day, when you ask, the favours will be returned. Those people with special skills or valuable knowledge are ideal for the bartering of favours.

7. Respect other people as individuals. This means understanding that they want things just as you do. If you know what they want and can convince them that your goals are compatible, you'll be a motivated team.

8. If you have to rely on power, harness power that everyone recognizes. Your power will increase if you do the following:
- Show the numbers. These are more compelling than opinions.
- Point to the precedent. Show others you are not guessing. If something has worked before, it will probably work again.
- Demonstrate the legitimacy.
- Point to ideas that have emanated from impeccable sources. Few people would then dare to challenge you. And, if they do, they will have little credibility.
- Present your ideas verbally. But the more formality you use — such as a PowerPoint presentation and a back-up report — the greater your chances of getting a "yes" response.

- Use logic. Nothing is more compelling than a sound argument. Make sure you have reason on your side. Present your supporting evidence whenever possible.
- Display expertise. If you have experience and knowledge, others will fall in behind you.
- Drum up mass support. If you can show that your ideas are shared by many, you can convince others that the ideas are sound.
- Create a rivalry. Nothing will bind your team together like the knowledge that they are competing with another group. Or present the possibility that another group is interested in your idea.

My idea of an agreeable person is a person who agrees with me.

SAM GOLDWYN, MOVIE MOGUL

Managing Your Time

I definitely am going to take a course on time management . . .
just as soon as I can work it into my schedule.

LOUIS BOONE (1914–65), AMERICAN CRITIC

*I*t might feel great to be busy all day long. But one needs to know that the time spent has been productive and not devoted to activities that will have little influence on sales and income. Great salespeople are ruthless about the use of their time. They are proactive and use a well-designed strategy to generate leads and sales. They set goals and then arrange daily activities to enable them to spend most of their time in revenue-generating activities.

1. Make every call count. Focus on those clients that are likely to give you the most business.

2. Save time by qualifying every prospect. As quickly as possible determine if the potential buyer
   • needs your product/service
   • can afford it
   • is an acceptable credit risk

3. Put a low priority on social calls. Certainly these visits are fun and have a low stress factor, but they don't put bread on the table. Perhaps you might indulge in such visits as an occasional "treat" after a very successful day.

4. Pace yourself. Don't try to do everything at once. Make a list of things that need to be done and allocate them to different days, depending on their need to get done.

5. Plan each day the afternoon or evening before. Doing this will give you the assurance that your day will be productive and enable you to have a good night's sleep.

6. If you are a travelling representative and depend on a vehicle, keep your car in tip-top condition. Driving a clean, dependable car will make you feel better about being on the road for many hours and will avoid the cost of unscheduled maintenance.

7. Demonstrate to your customers how concerned you are about time — yours and theirs. Have an agenda at meetings. Tell the potential customer what you would like to achieve, how to get there, and how long it should take.

8. Keep healthy. Look after yourself. Eat well and exercise. It will make you feel wonderful about yourself and increase your confidence and sales.

9. Take vacations. Sure, time away from work is costly, but it is necessary. Time away from the office will give you time to charge your batteries, and to think about what you are doing and the things you could be doing better.

10. If you're always busy and never accomplishing the things you need done, you are either doing the wrong things or doing the right things inefficiently. The first step is to make a list of things that have to get done (leaving room for unforeseen contingencies). Do everything on the list — and don't do the things that are not on it.

11. Rank the things on your list according to the following criteria:
- anything relating to existing or potential customers
- anything important to your reputation within the company
- anything deferrable or social

Act upon them in the order outlined above.

12. When you're working down your list, do one thing at a time. Don't worry about the next items. This will only slow you down.

13. Take advantage of every available moment to get things done. Are you doing all of the following?
- using a cell phone to optimize travel time
- using e-mail — including portable e-mail — to ensure swift and easy response to issues as they arise
- taking public transit to give you time to go through minor paperwork
- coming to meetings with an agenda. The hit-or-miss approach wastes time.
- keeping up with your professional development at opportune times. Keep important articles with you. Read them when you're waiting for a client or standing in line.
- working from a convenient location. If you're spending hours commuting, you're squandering productivity.

14. Don't let meetings eat up your time.
- Set an example by showing up on time. And starting on time. Reward promptness rather than tardiness.
- Establish a time for the meeting to end. If you are not in charge, ask the chair. Doing so will encourage everyone to stay focused.
- Ask permission to leave when agenda items do not concern you. There is no point wasting your time or the company's time.
- Be the time-cop, that is, the timekeeper. It will be your job to blow the whistle when speakers are using more than their allotted time on an agenda item.

15. Don't let others waste the time that you have carefully saved. Social chatter costs you money and opportunity. Here's how to avoid time-wasters without giving offence.
- Limit social contact to lunch or some other established time. Social time is important. It unclogs the mind and eases communication with others. Just don't overdo it.
- Make your office a sanctuary. Do you have a secretary? Ask him or her to guard the door. If you don't, keep your door closed when you have something important to do.
- Get out of your chair when a time-waster arrives. This will prevent him or her from sitting down for a long conversation.
- Just as you seek eye contact with those you want to show interest in, avoid eye contact with those you do not want to encourage.

16. Use your environment to your advantage.
- Try not to meet people in your office. That way you can end a meeting without giving offence.

- Don't invite chit-chatters into your space. If you have comfortable chairs arrayed around your desk, you are encouraging others to sit. Get rid of the chairs.
- Sit so that you're not facing other people. This will discourage idle conversation.
- Find the ideal location for your desk. Try to save time by moving close to the people you work with and away from social traffic.

17. Don't exhaust yourself. You don't work well when you're cramped and tired.
- Take breaks to stretch and unclutter your mind.
- Exercise.

18. Work during quiet times. Can you come in early or leave late?

19. Use a time-saving device like a day-timer or similar software. Look for the following features:
- calendar and "to-do" sections
- in the case of software, on-screen reminders, schedule-sharing, and integrated e-mail

11
Organizational
Effectiveness

Surviving Office Politics

Great minds discuss ideas; average minds discuss events; small minds discuss people.

ELEANOR ROOSEVELT (1884–1962), AMERICAN HUMANITARIAN

Sometimes the office feels like a soap opera: cunning, deceit, and mutual distrust make the workday feel like high drama. But it can also destroy the team spirit and sap the company's strength. Even if you are often away from the office, you can still be drawn into the intrigue and bickering. Here are some strategies to keep yourself above the fray.

1. Perhaps it's not such a big deal after all. At the very least this approach will prevent you from getting sucked into petty squabbles. At best it will show your even-handedness.

2. Look for compromise. A solution may be staring everyone in the face, ignored because both sides are fighting too bitterly. Be the person to see the common ground.

3. Know when to laugh. It can make much of the bitterness disappear.

4. Focus your criticism on issues rather than people. And never stoop to insult. This only makes compromise impossible. No one will ever say, "You're right, I'm stupid." But they may say, "You're right, things just might work more efficiently if . . ." Give them that opportunity.

5. A principal rule is that you can never really be neutral. You'll just end up being resented by both sides. Learn to play the game right if you have to.

6. Pick the winning side. Among other things, this means never going it alone. Don't go against the grain and do not choose adversaries more powerful than you. Find out what the senior players are thinking. Go with them unless their position is morally untenable.

7. Don't join a splinter group against your boss. For one thing, your plot could come back to haunt you. For another, it's just not the right thing to do. Hopefully the two of you have been working hard to establish trust. Don't squander that for short-term gain.

8. Don't join a group that is working against the interests of your company. Again, it is a violation of trust that will be difficult to mend.

9. Ally yourself only with people with similar values. More cynical alliances will be short and can quickly turn sour.

10. Look for signs that your ship is sinking. If it is, don't jump to the other ship. You'll only annoy everyone. Now is the time to claim the privileges of neutrality. Another rule is to always try to fight fair. You may be playing for keeps (or you may not), but playing dirty can backfire badly. And it will usually cost you the respect of your peers and superiors. Always keep your head.

11. Try to look at the issue from the perspective of the other side. How would you feel if you were on that side? Perhaps they have a point.

Selling Ideas
to Your Boss

Nothing can take the place of persistence.
Talent will not; nothing is more common than
unsuccessful men with talent.
Genius will not; unrewarded genius is a proverb.
Education will not; the world is full of educated failures.
Keep believing.
Keep trying.
Persistence and determination alone are omnipotent.

CALVIN COOLIDGE (1872–1933), 30TH PRESIDENT OF THE UNITED STATES

What's the point in having great ideas if you can't sell them to the people who control their implementation? And if you never see your idea implemented, how much satisfaction will you derive from it? Here are some ideas that will increase the odds of getting approval for your project.

1. Before you meet with a potential sponsor, be prepared.
  • Pick your best ideas. Don't try to sell every one. Choose those that
    – are in line with the organization's mission

- have a reasonable chance of being accepted
- are the ones you feel most passionate about
- Collect as much information as possible to support
  your position. Facts speak louder than words.
- Find examples of a similar idea that might have worked
  elsewhere. This will enable you to demonstrate a precedent.
- Don't rely on presenting your ideas verbally. Collect them in
  documented form. Doing this will add legitimacy to your
  position. Colour brochures of the equipment you want to
  buy or expert endorsements in credible trade or business
  magazines will enhance your position.
- Make people aware of the possibility that a competitor may
  use your idea. This sense of rivalry may spur your sponsor
  to action in hopes of staying one step ahead.
- Be prepared to talk the language of your audience. If you
  are dealing with the management, are you ready to show a
  cost benefit? Can you prove to human resources people some
  measurable benefit to improve morale?

2. When you are making your pitch, do the following:
- Greet the person(s) warmly. Thank them for their time.
- Let them know your expected outcome. Be specific and
  assertive. Speak with a firm voice that emphasizes key results.
- Be positive. Saying "I expect to come away from this meeting
  with approval to start a pilot project" is better than "I hope
  you'll like my idea . . . perhaps, maybe, you'll let me try it."
- Don't exaggerate the benefits. Be optimistic yet realistic.
- Give them a chance to ask questions. Listen carefully to what
  they have to say. Answer them or offer to get back to them if
  the answer requires further thought or research.
- When your presentation is done, be silent. Wait till you get

a "buying signal" such as "When can you start?" or "Do you
think we can manage given our lack of time?" Then assure
them of success and show them your timetable.

- Don't ask for approval in a way that allows them to say "no."
  Replace "Can we go ahead?" with "Do you have any other
  ideas that would ensure success?" or "When do you think we
  should start?" or "When would you like the project to be
  completed by?"

Working with a
Difficult Boss

*I don't want any "Yes-men" around me.
I want everyone to tell me the truth,
even if it costs them their jobs.*

SAM GOLDWYN, MOVIE MOGUL

If something isn't working out in your career, the thing to do is change it. However, your boss is one of the few things that you cannot change. What you can change is the nature of your relationship with him. This may be difficult, since you are not in a position of great power. After all, it is your job to please your boss, while your boss has no such responsibility to you. Still, a good relationship will probably be advantageous to both of you. That is your starting point.

1. Start by getting rid of whatever resentment you may have. It will do you no good. Instead, remember that no boss is going to be ideal. Work with what you have.

2. Never forget the power your boss has over you. If you are feeling rebellious, keep in mind that this power does not evaporate even if you quit — your new boss will probably want a reference. So don't let your differences escalate into open war.

3. Remember that any blame is probably shared. Think hard about this. Have you done anything to exacerbate the situation? Try to see things from your boss's point of view. This will enable you to be the problem-solver rather than the problem-starter. Take responsibility for positive change.

4. Never give into the temptation to say bad things about your boss when he is not around. That kind of talk has a way of getting back. And when it does, there will be a price to pay. You will have lost your boss's trust.

5. Keep your boss's interests in mind at all times. You have nothing to gain by embarrassing him, even if you derive a little malicious satisfaction. If your boss asks you to do something that you know will not work out, make the problem your own. Ensuring that the matter is dealt with satisfactorily will show your responsibility and gain valuable trust.

6. If your differences come to a head, be proactive. Arrange a talk to air things out. Here's what to keep in mind.
- Keep your differences private. Meet away from your co-workers, either behind closed doors or in a restaurant. If your conflict becomes public, your boss will have no room to back down.
- Focus on issues, not personalities. Especially avoid the pronoun "you." Using "I" should side-step the matter of blame. Try something like "I find it difficult to use my time efficiently when I don't know what I am going to be doing for the day. I want to get as much done as possible, but it is hard when I am always juggling unexpected tasks."
- Always strive for solutions instead of dwelling on problems.

You will give your boss the opportunity to suggest improvements if you ask for advice. Ask, "How can I improve this situation?"

7. Try to "train" your boss just as he trains you. Provide positive reinforcement. When your boss does something to improve the situation, show your appreciation — and work harder. Things will keep improving.

8. The final solution, if it is a solution, is to leave. You might try a different division of your company. Or you might quit altogether. Either way, try not to leave on a bad note. If you fault your boss for everything, you'll look bitter. Stay cool and professional.

Stress Management

*Adopting the right attitude can convert a
negative stress into a positive one.*

HANS SELYE (1907–82), AUSTRIAN-CANADIAN ENDOCRINOLOGIST

*A*s a salesperson, you are under enormous pressure to produce. You are at the beginning of the sales cycle, in the middle if things go wrong, and at the end if expectations are not met. You need to ensure that your stress levels are in check so you can put your best foot forward at all times. Here are some things you can do to maintain equilibrium.

1. Take an active approach to stress. Right away, this means that if you can't do anything to change the situation, don't stress about it! Does bumper-to-bumper traffic enrage you? If so, you're getting worked up over nothing. Relax. The same goes for late flights, long line-ups, busy signals, and other things over which you have no control.

2. Walk away. Go for a walk. If a problem is driving you up the wall, take a moment to cool down and consider what, if anything, is to be done. The problem will seem simpler when you return.

3. Give yourself a break when things get too demanding. Turn the lights off in your office, or just close your eyes. Better yet, keep an eye-guard handy to shut out the world for a few moments. Imagine a place where you have no choice but to relax: a tropical beach, a quiet cottage afternoon.

4. Get some shut-eye. A 15-minute nap will put gas in the tank. But don't sleep much longer than that or you'll wake up groggy.

5. Try some meditation techniques to clear your mind. Repeat a mantra in your mind. You will soon feel the immediate demands of the day slipping away.

6. Indulge yourself a little. Take a long hot bath with some scented oils or soothing salts. Or get a massage. A proper massage will not only your invigorate body, but also clear your mind.

7. Go for a workout. Exercise will not only allow you to blow off steam, it will keep you feeling good. If you're fit, you'll have armour against stress.

8. Pay attention to what your body is telling you. Are your shoulders cramped? Is your back sore? Are you hunched over your desk? If so, you are an easy victim for stress. Stretch your knotted muscles and your stress will fall away.

9. Value your friends. A sympathetic listener will help you unburden, see things more clearly. And, perhaps most importantly, allow you to see that your problems are not so huge after all.

10. Don't get caught up in a moment of negativity. Take stock. Remember, there are plenty of good things in your life, and lots of people are worse off than you. Balance whatever is bothering you now with all of your blessings. Things aren't really so bad.

11. Don't rely on toxins to soothe you. Sure, a drink or a smoke (or something illegal) may be tempting. And it may improve your mood short-term. But these chemicals are addictive and may make your problems worse. Consider trying herbal and naturopathic products to improve your mood instead.

12. Is stress keeping you up at night? If so
- avoid going to bed late
- try drinking camomile tea (or the classic warm milk — it works!)
- soak in a hot bath before slipping between cool sheets

Don't take your troubles to bed with you. If you are angry or hurt, air your problem before you turn in. You'll sleep better and feel better.

13. Don't wear yourself out. The source of your stress may not be the world around you. It could be your own bad habits. Do you
- expect perfection consistently?
- refuse to delegate responsibility?
- withhold trust from those you count on?
- assign blame unfairly (to yourself and others)?
- find yourself losing your temper?
- work yourself to the bone without seeing the results you expect?

If you answered *yes* to many of these questions, you probably expect too much of yourself and are doomed to frustrate yourself.

It is good to be ambitious, but counterproductive and even destructive to set impossible goals and pursue them relentlessly. Take a step back.

I went on a diet, swore off drinking and heavy eating. In 14 days I had lost exactly two weeks.

JOE E. LEWIS (1902–71), AMERICAN COMEDIAN, ACTOR

12

Personal
Development

Learning:

Getting the Most out of Workshops

Education's purpose is to replace an empty mind with an open one.

MALCOLM FORBES (1919–90), AMERICAN PUBLISHER

$\mathcal{T}$here are many ways to develop yourself: mentoring, peer coaching, workshops, conferences, self-study, to name a few. Whatever combination of strategies you choose, it is always important to bear in mind what constitutes success, particularly in a formalized training situation.

Ultimately, learning is not about what happens in the classroom. It is about how the student's new skills and knowledge are applied in the real world. Does he or she actually use what has been learned? Does he or she show an increase in performance on the job? This is what learning is all about. Here's how to ensure that this happens for you:

1. First, do you actually need formal training, or is there a better way to develop new skills? Consider
- learning on the job from a colleague or senior employee
- consulting a manual or a self-help book
- researching the material on the Internet
- learning from developmental software

2. If you determine that a workshop is the way to go, find out whether your organization offers in-house training. Such training has many benefits:

- The material will be tailored to your organization and the learning experience will be shared by people you work with. This will make the new skills much easier to put into practice.
- You will have a network of "trouble-shooters" at work with you. Your workday will be an ongoing study group.
- You and your company will waste less valuable work time.
- If management organizes the workshop, it may be in anticipation of an upcoming challenge. You'll be prepared for exactly what the company is going to throw at you.

3. There are also advantages to attending a workshop outside of what your company offers. For example:

- You'll be able to get a broader perspective. Just as an in-house workshop will prepare you for exactly what your company is doing, an outside learning experience will get you up to speed on what everybody else is doing.
- You'll have a chance to network. This can not only give you valuable contacts, it can also teach you what you have in common with others in your field. And it may suggest unusual approaches to common problems, things that you and your organization hadn't thought of.

4. Prepare for the workshop.

- Think about how you learn. People have different preferred learning styles, such as
  - looking at examples and visual displays
  - listening to understand theory and abstraction
  - participating in activities and role play

- Does the workshop you're interested in fit with your preferred learning style? If not, could you reinforce your learning with homework that will fit your own style (and are you ready to do the extra work involved)?
- Research the instructor. What can you find out about his credentials? his teaching style? This will help you be ready for situations you might otherwise stumble in.
- Know what you want. Have questions ready. Be proactive. Everyone will appreciate it — you, your instructor, and your classmates.

5. There is a great deal you can do to improve the learning experience while you're in the classroom.
- Stay focused on your objectives. Highlight material as it is presented. Ask questions to keep the instructor focused on what matters to you.
- Approach the instructor during breaks if you feel that your questions are going in a direction that others have little interest in. He will probably be happy to talk to you, impressed with your keen interest, and relieved to have a quiet moment to discuss such matters away from the class.
- Keep quality notes. Summarize as you go and at the end of the day. This will force you to put things in your own words — which forces you to understand.
- Don't hang back. Participation enables you to put new knowledge into practice.
- Sit close to the front.
- Don't be afraid of feedback — ask for it! And don't be too sensitive if you don't get things right the first time. Think about it. What if you had gone back to work and made that mistake there? You're just getting the bugs out of the system.

- Don't be afraid to try new things. Push yourself to the limits. This is the place to do it, since there is no penalty for failure.
- Look for someone you can trust and keep in touch with. You will be able to turn to each other for support and practical advice later. Arrange your first meeting before you part ways.
- Find some way to present your new knowledge to your boss when you get back. Just as summarizing the material for yourself forced you to fully internalize it, presenting it under a little bit of pressure will help you nail the salient points even more.

Attitude

What the caterpillar calls the end of the world,
the master calls a butterfly.

RICHARD BACH, AMERICAN NOVELIST

*S*uccess comes from having a great attitude first. These key components are part of the attitude of any successful salesperson, and they should become part of your mantra.

1. Work hard. Be dedicated to your task. Start preparing each day early and work till the job is done.

2. Love to sell. Love what you do. Be enthusiastic and passionate about the value you bring.

3. Seldom quit. Quitting on the first rebuff or at the first hurdle is an indication you should switch careers.

4. Be eternally optimistic. Look at setbacks as temporary, with better things surely ahead. The glass is always half full and never half empty.

5. Be knowledgeable. Know your product capabilities and specifications inside out. Also, know the industry and competitive products and services intimately.

6. Never stop learning. Learn from
  - your mistakes
  - courses
  - customers
  - reading
  - trade shows
  - sales and industry magazines (get subscriptions!)

7. Be enthusiastic. Show excitement about your profession, your organization, and what you offer to your clients.

8. Be empathetic. Understand the point of view of the customer. Put yourself in your customers' shoes and devise solutions that will benefit them.

9. Be a believer. See good in yourself, your family, your products, your company, and your customers.

10. Be self-confident. Wake up each day, look in the mirror and say, "You're wonderful!"

11. Have high energy. Get things done with gusto. Don't procrastinate even if the task at hand is difficult. Never say *someday*. In fact, tomorrow is today!

12. Arrange your time ruthlessly. Understand the Pareto principle: 80 percent of your success comes from 20 percent of your activities. So allow those activities to take 80 percent of your time. Delegate activities that don't contribute directly or indirectly to sales.

13. Have a sense of humour. Salespeople are likeable because they see the lighter side of life. Always wear a smile, laugh easily, and enjoy listening to or telling a good story. Make sure your jokes are always tasteful.

14. Project a sense of pride when representing the organization.

Yesterday is history. Tomorrow is a mystery. Today is a gift.

ELEANOR ROOSEVELT (1884–1962), AMERICAN HUMANITARIAN

Job Interviews

You never get a second chance to make a first impression.

I don't advocate changing jobs often, particularly if the reasons causing you to leave are tolerable. Each employer will have things you don't appreciate. But, if an opportunity arises for a significant promotion, more responsibility, and significantly higher remuneration, it would be in your interests to investigate.

If you have a job interview scheduled, you have probably already done a great deal of work. You were researching and networking and strategizing before you even applied for the new position. Your interview is your chance to put all of this to good use — and to put it all on the line! Don't let it go to waste. You won't get the job by smiling and offering a few clichéd phrases. You will probably be talking to a human resources specialist. So you need to be prepared.

BEFORE THE BIG DAY

1. You should have already looked into the company before applying. But keep in mind that an in-depth knowledge of

the company will impress your interviewer with your ability to
plan ahead and your enthusiasm for the company. Have this
knowledge at your disposal:

- What kind of business is the company in?
- Is the company doing well?
- Are there important issues in the industry for you to keep
  abreast of?
- How big is the company?
- Are you familiar with the range of their products?

2. Interviewers will expect you to ask questions, so have some ready.
Naturally, you will want to talk about your salary, but avoid
bringing this up too early. You don't want to seem too money-
oriented. Ask questions about how you can contribute to the
organization. Ask

- what the company's plans are for the next five years
- what the corporate culture is like
- how performance is rewarded, apart from salary bonuses
- whether teamwork is an important element in day-to-day
  operations
- how employees are alerted to changes in the company
- why people have left in the past few years
- what employees of the organization have in common

3. Polish your resumé. Tailor it to the needs of the organization
to which you are applying. Know what you have to offer.

4. Schedule your appointment so that you won't have to rush to or
from the interview. You don't want to be late and you don't want
to be in a hurry to leave.

5. Assemble all of your credentials and references. Saying "references available upon request" is only making the interviewer's job more difficult.

6. Make sure you know exactly where you are going. You don't want to show up late and have to explain that you couldn't find the building or that there were no parking spots available.

7. Practise your interviewing skills with someone you trust. She will be the interviewer and throw questions at you. She can then give you feedback on your verbal and non-verbal performance. Your practice questions should be something like these:
- What would your boss say is your greatest weakness?
- What was the high point of your last job?
- How would you describe yourself?
- What kind of training could you undertake to improve your performance?
- What is it about this job that made you want to apply?
- What qualification can you tell me about that is not on your resumé?
- Can you give me an example of a situation in your last job that showed leadership and commitment? What is it?

ON THE BIG DAY

1. Dress the part.
- Have pressed clothes ready for the day. Make sure your shoes are shined. Get a nice haircut. It's a sound investment.
- Know beforehand what the dress code is. You want to look like you belong. When in doubt, dress up rather than down.

- Don't go for excessive fashion statements or obviously "sexy" outfits. You're trying to fit in, not stand out.

2. Give yourself lots of time to get to the interview. Be early. Take the time to visualize yourself being successful.

3. Make sure you have all your papers with you, including your certification, your resumé, a portfolio perhaps, and anything else you may need.

4. Carry a pen and notepad with you. You will be discussing important things. Don't assume you'll remember everything.

5. Let your "people" skills break the ice. Introduce yourself with a firm handshake and a sincere smile. Start with some light conversation. "I love the design of your head office. There is so much natural light. It makes the working environment so pleasant!"

6. Be confident but quiet. Listen actively to the questions posed by the interviewer, rephrasing them from time to time to make it clear that you understand.

7. Be careful with open-ended questions. You will have practised your answers. Stick to responses that offer clear and direct information. If you're nervous you may be inclined to ramble on and on. Be wary of this.

8. Communicate your confidence and interest with your body language. Maintain eye contact. Lean slightly forward. Smile and nod gently. Sit without fidgeting.

9. Watch the interviewer's body language. Is he or she manifesting confusion? boredom? resistance? That is, have you lost eye contact? Has her face gone blank? Are her arms crossed? These cues will tell you when to change your approach.

10. Present yourself as an attractive employee. This means showing enthusiasm and energy. Focus on the positive and give examples of behaviour that shows this attitude.

11. Since your voice is your primary medium in the interview, make sure it sends the right message.
  • Enunciate clearly.
  • Speak firmly when you come to important moments.
  • Be careful you don't slip into slang or profanity. And avoid unguarded idiom, such as "so she was, like, what*ever*."

12. Just as you speak carefully, listen carefully. If you don't listen carefully, you can't be certain that you have answered the question fully. If you are unsure, ask. Don't be afraid. Your question will demonstrate your desire to understand and communicate.

13. Paraphrase important questions back to the interviewer. This will demonstrate understanding, interest, and listening.

14. Back yourself up with examples. If your interviewer can imagine you on the job, you are one step closer to getting it.

15. Don't end the meeting up in the air. Begin the next stage of communication. You might ask something like "What is the next step?" And be sure to end politely. If you're nervous you may want to sprint for the door. Don't. Say "nice to meet you," as you would with anyone else.

BE READY FOR THESE QUESTIONS

Interviewers evaluate potential employees by asking a standard set of questions. You can be sure that some of the questions below will be asked at your interview. Make sure you have answers!

- What is your greatest achievement in the last year?
- Tell me about your worst blunder at work.
- If you could create your own position, what would it be?
- If you could design or organize a company, how would you do it?
- What are the elements of the work environment that annoy you most?
- What motivates you?
- What do you expect from this position/company that you did not get in your last job?
- What would your colleagues/boss describe as your best quality?
- What would they say is your greatest fault?

Self-Confidence

The only place where success comes before work is the dictionary.

VIDAL SASSOON

A salesperson needs self-confidence as much as he or she needs a product to sell. And just as you have to believe in your product, you have to believe in yourself. Are you a risk-taker? Are you willing to take on challenging projects? Do you have what it takes to speak your mind in public? These are the marks of a confident salesperson. We can all improve our confidence levels. Here's how:

1. Cheer yourself on. Be your biggest supporter. Tell yourself you're terrific when you get out of the car in the morning.

2. Present a positive face not only to others but also to yourself. Smile when you look in the mirror and tell yourself how great you are.

3. Give yourself some positive reinforcement. Celebrate every success, even if it is not a monumental achievement. It may only be a cup of coffee, but you'll be training yourself to succeed.

4. Don't leave things to nag you. Whatever you're doing, finish it. And do your very best, no matter what it is. Leaving little things undone or poorly done will sap your sense of progress and triumph.

5. Look for evidence of your effort and achievement. Ask your boss or your peers how you're doing. If you're trying, they'll acknowledge it and give you a boost.

6. Never stagnate. Laziness will drag you down. Learn new things and put them to work for you. The results will buoy you up.

Finding the
Right Mentor

*Mentoring is about giving gifts – gifts of confidence,
encouragement and respect.*

ELIZABETH HOYLE, VP MARKETING, TRIMARK INVESTMENTS

Life and work are often frustrating. Most people have the ability to deal with the unexpected challenges that face us. But sometimes we don't cope all that well. In some situations, we can benefit from the advice of someone who can see things from a different perspective or who has experienced a similar situation before.

The right mentor may not be immediately obvious. There are lots of intelligent, experienced people who know what they're talking about. But they might not be right for you. Ending up with the wrong mentor can slow down your career, so keep your eyes open and look for someone with just the right qualities.

An effective mentor will have these qualities:

- *She listens without making judgements.* She acts as a sounding board and allows you to come to your own conclusions if you are unable to solve a problem.

- *She is not needy or vain.* Such people will want to mould you in their image. A good teacher has nothing to prove.
- *He communicates clearly and honestly.* You want a straight shooter who gives meaningful feedback.
- *He keeps things upbeat.* If your mentor has lots of positive energy, you'll be able to learn more and enjoy the process.
- *She respects you as a person.* If you are just a chore for your mentor, you will not get the best from her.
- *She is open-minded.* Remember that you have plenty to offer. A good mentor should value that and learn from you. She will not only talk but listen.
- *He wants to see you succeed.*
- *He keeps the process challenging.* The best way to learn is to be walked through the decision-making process. A good mentor will not simply give you all the answers. Instead, he will respond with another question, even if it is simply, "First, what do you think?"
- *She outranks you.* If your mentor is your senior, she will have a "higher" perspective and will see the big picture. That is the perspective you want to have.
- *She has other unique perspectives.* For example, if your mentor works in a different department, she will know and see things that you don't. A more experienced mentor will have been through situations you have not.

Finding the right mentor is not easy. Talk to your human resources department about your needs. They will probably have some ideas about who would be willing to spend some time with you.

Problem Solving —
The Top 10 Principles

Most people would rather die than think; in fact, they do so.

BERTRAND RUSSELL (1872–1970), BRITISH PHILOSOPHER

$\mathcal{S}$ alespeople are sandwiched between the client and the organization they represent. They are seen as having the answers to problems that arise on either side. Apart from having wonderful interpersonal skills to manage conflict and anger, they need to be able to solve problems systematically, one at a time, so that the issues do not keep resurfacing.

While every problem is different and requires its own solution, there are techniques that apply to solving any problem that can arise:

1. Don't try to do everything at once. Solve your problems one at a time, starting with the most important. Work your way down the list. You will probably find that only one or two of your problems are significant and that the rest just make the situation look worse than it really is.

2. Solve only problems that can be solved. People waste precious energy fretting over things they cannot control. Focus on things that can be done and your efforts will have an immediate effect.

3. Don't go looking for problems until you are quite sure you have none of your own to worry about. Some problems will require the intervention of others, usually senior management. Leave such concerns until you can focus your attention on them. Or let them go. Besides, solutions over which you have exclusive control are the easiest. Get them out of the way first.

4. Don't try to solve a problem in one fell swoop (unless it is small and trivial). Follow a process. This is how mathematicians solve their problems. Don't make hasty decisions that yield only temporary solutions.

5. Get your facts straight. The wrong solution is as bad as another problem, so be sure your answers don't make things worse. The best way to ensure you have the right solution is to be certain that you have the right problem.

6. Don't try to do everything yourself. There are lots of people in your company who have an interest in seeing the problems solved — and some of them are paid to solve them. Get these people on board. Look for people who have these characteristics:
- *An eye for detail.* Sloppy people will create more problems.
- *The potential to come up with creative ideas.* You want a fresh approach.
- *An ability to work well with others.* People who clash with others engender as many problems as they solve — if they solve any.

7. Don't remake old mistakes. If old solutions worked, old problems wouldn't be popping up again. You need new ideas, so don't be afraid to try them. Moreover, if an idea is yours, you will get credit for it and may end up in a leadership role when it comes time to implement it.

8. Solicit the perspectives of new employees. They will not be blinded by the habits of people who have been around a long time. They may have a solution that has been staring you in the face all the while.

9. Understand the problem. You can't solve it until you know exactly what it is. This means making sure that you
- address the cause, not the symptom
- look at every possible cause
- tailor your solution to the well-defined cause
- look for fresh approaches

10. Have a carefully planned strategy. Leave nothing to chance. Put your solution into practice. Follow your plan.

Stand back and watch. And when your solution is successful, celebrate!

Index

acceptance, 83–84
advancement, 212–16
advertising. *See* handouts;
    testimonials
agreement, 152–53, 173
appearance. *See* dress
appointments. *See* meetings
arrogance, 79
articles, 50
attention, 78, 88–89
attitude, 18, 26, 75, 243, 253–55
audience, 118, 121
awards, 56–57

body language, 26, 102, 119
    reading, 71–72, 83–87, 90
    responding to, 84–86, 140, 150
    using, 87, 89, 127, 259–60
boss
    difficult, 239–41
    relationship with, 214–15, 234
    selling ideas to, 236–38
breaks, 230, 243
brochures, 31, 47
business cards, 25, 47, 51, 54, 58
buyers, 10, 38–39, 150

case studies, 46, 57, 103
cell phones, 38, 187, 228
chain of command, 78, 220
chat rooms, 193
clarification, 89, 90, 103, 128
client relations, 12, 166–69, 177–79
closing sales, 18, 70, 85, 86, 149–51,
    152–58
cold calls, 30–34
communication, 139–41, 186–87.
    See also e-mail
commuting, 228
competition, 103, 130
competitors, 199, 237
computers, 186, 195
concessions, 151
conferences, 45–47
confidence, 26, 87, 120–21, 254, 259,
    262–63
confidentiality, 218
confirmation, 104, 125, 139, 140, 145
conflicts, 213, 219, 224, 239–41, 267
contacts, 11, 18, 22, 25
    pursuing, 27, 43, 51–52
contests, 56–57, 219
conversations, 57. *See also* networking

copyright, 219
cost reduction, 40
courses. *See* training
creativity, 221, 222
credibility, 74, 224–25
criticism, 214, 234
cultural differences, 58, 71, 83, 141
customers, 5–6, 8, 18, 51
  needs of, 68, 93–95
  relationship with, 166–69, 177–79
customer service, 3–6, 76, 175, 222

decision-makers, 10, 55, 107
demonstrations, 115–16
digital cameras, 186
documentation, 167, 168, 174, 237.
  See also case studies; reference letters;
  testimonials
document sharing, 173
dress, 4, 26, 72–73, 77, 216, 222
  for job interviews, 258–59
dumping, 79

EASI (electronic assisted sales integration),
  170–73
electronic tools, 29, 171
e-mail, 36, 39, 60, 75, 143, 173, 189–91,
  228
empathy, 75, 144, 254
enemies, 215
enthusiasm, 72, 77, 87, 121, 253.
  See also attitude
  showing, 26, 222, 254, 260
equipment buying, 184, 187
ethics, 217–20
exaggeration, 77
exercise, 230, 243
expectations, 244–45
eye contact, 71, 89, 126, 139, 229,
  259–60

fairness, 218, 219, 235
favours, 224
faxing, 143, 187
feedback, 17, 143
  receiving, 23, 63, 150, 215, 251, 265
  for self-evaluation, 214, 215, 258, 263
file-sharing, 188
follow-up, 27, 47, 145, 156
  after trade shows, 51, 56, 59–61
force-field analysis, 206–7
free offers, 21
friends, 243

gatekeepers, 11
goal setting, 8–9, 49, 175, 203–7

handouts, 37, 47, 54.
  See also samples
handshakes, 26, 71
harassment, 78
health, 227
honesty, 217–20
humour, 233, 254, 255

influence, 10–12, 129–31
Internet, 186–89, 192–99
interruptions, 89, 229–30
interviews, 256–61
intranets, 188
introductions, 20, 24, 33, 67–68
issues, 105–10, 145

job change, 208–11, 256–61

knowledge, 26, 74–75, 254
  demonstrating, 121, 130

language, 22, 23, 29, 99–100, 116, 141, 260.
  See also body language; non-verbal
  communication

learning, 53–55, 249–52, 254. *See also* training

legitimacy, 103, 130, 131

letters, 19–23, 47, 56. *See also* mailings

listening, 26, 79, 87–92, 140, 141, 144, 260

  in negotiations, 125, 127

  in telephone calls, 34, 61

literature, 31, 47, 57. *See also* handouts

loyalty, 218, 220, 234

mailings, 19–23, 30, 31, 35, 36, 56. *See also* e-mail

meals, 54

media, 50

meditation, 243

meetings, 43, 51, 59, 171, 176, 188, 229

  agendas for, 227, 228

  setting up, 30, 34, 50–51, 61

mentors, 215, 264–65

misrepresentation, 219

mission statements, 176, 203, 205–6

moonlighting, 218

motivation, 22

negotiating, 124–31, 173

networking, 24–27, 40, 250

  at trade shows, 48–52, 54–55

newsletters, 28–29

non-verbal communication, 68, 140. *See also* body language

note-taking, 58, 90

objections, 69, 70, 99–107

open-ended questions, 25, 63, 72, 90, 105, 125

  to determine customer needs, 68, 140

  in telephone calls, 34, 44

  opening, 67–68. *See also* introductions

optimism, 253

peers, 215, 223–25

people skills, 142–45

performance, 8, 9, 175

performance management systems, 168

persistence, 17, 130

personal information management system (PIMS), 185–86

personality types, 135–38

pilot projects, 172, 173, 237

planning, 49, 55, 213, 227

politics, 233–35

power, 223, 224–25

precedent, 103, 129, 130, 224, 237

prejudice, 218

presentations, 35–37, 45–47, 49–50, 113–24

  apologizing for, 156–57

  to boss, 236–38

press releases, 50

pressure tactics, 78, 140

pricing, 108–10

prioritizing, 266

problem solving, 266–68

process improvement, 174–75

procrastination, 221

products, 8, 23, 69, 70, 122–23, 150–51, 237

professional development, 228. *See also* training

professionalism, 76, 221–22

progress tracking, 213

promotion, 198–99

prospect evaluation, 15–16, 40, 55, 93–95, 226

questions, 79, 102, 127, 141, 150, 261, 265. *See also* open-ended questions

  confirming, 104, 139, 140, 145

rank, 131

rationality, 103, 131

rebates, 103
receptionists, 39
reference letters, 22, 103, 130, 258
referrals, 18, 33–34, 40–44, 54, 140
reliability, 75, 78
research, 102, 192–93
respect, 223–24
resumé, 257
rewards, 168, 176, 207
risk, 103
roadblocks, 205, 206, 221

sales, 17–18, 161–63, 173, 205, 206
sales presentations, 113–23
samples, 21, 62–63
search engines, 199
self-confidence. *See* confidence
selling, 67–70, 161–63
    of ideas, 236–38
    partnership for, 163–79
sharing, 188, 215
skills, 208, 209, 249
sleep, 243, 244
socializing, 227, 229–30
software, 173, 184, 196, 230
spam, 189, 191
speakers, 36, 58
speeches, 45–47, 49–50, 58. *See also*
    presentations
storefront (Internet), 188
stress, 242–45
supply chain, 170–73

teaching, 213
teams, 173, 174–77
teamwork, 213, 224–25
teaser copy, 22–23
technology, 170–73, 183–99
telephone, 33, 38–39, 50.
    See also cell phones
telephone calls, 30, 43, 44, 60–61, 188.
    See also cold calls; voice mail
testimonials, 21, 37, 46, 57
thanking, 37, 43, 215
time management, 221–22, 226–30,
    255
timing, 43, 150
to-do list, 228
trade shows, 48–61
training, 205, 214, 250–52
trust, 234, 240

URL. *See* Web sites

vacations, 227
values, 204, 208–9, 234
vehicle, 227
vision statement, 203
voice conferencing, 173
voice mail, 38–39, 187
volunteering, 25, 50, 213

Web sites, 188–89, 194–97, 199
whiteboards, 171, 173
workshops. *See* training